Lace Collection

FOR KNITTING

Lace Collection

FOR KNITTING

Intricate Shawls, Simple Accessories,
Cozy Sweaters and More Stylish Designs
for Every Season

Design Originals

an Imprint of Fox Chapel Publishing
www.d-originals.com

LACE
COLLECTION

WELCOME

TO LACE COLLECTION FOR KNITTING!

Whether you're a lace knitting expert or have always wanted to be, there's plenty to inspire in this collection of projects. Inside you'll find pages full of ideas for creative lace knitting, with over 20 beautiful patterns from some of the world's top lace designers. If you are new to lace knitting, or need a refresher, included are helpful guides on crochet techniques, lace yarns, creating the perfect lace with the perfect finish, and how to care for your finished pieces. Once you've browsed the gorgeous designs, like the Abruzzi Capelet (page 47), and the Virginia Set (page 82), you will be inspired to create your own lovely lace pieces.

Abbreviations

alt	alternate	**M1**	make one (inc 1 stitch)	**pm**	place marker	**SSP**	slip 2 sts one at a time, purl 2 slipped stitches together tbl
approx	approximately			**prev**	previous		
beg	beginning	**M1L**	Left leaning inc. With left needle tip, lift strand between needles from front to back. Knit lifted loop through back of loop.	**psso**	pass slipped stitch over		
cn	cable needle					**st(s)**	stitch(es)
cont	continue			**P2tog**	purl 2 stitches together	**st st**	stockinette stitch
dc	double crochet (US single crochet)					**tbl**	through back of the loop
				P3tog	purl 3 stitches together		
dec	decrease (work two stitches together)	**M1R**	Right leaning inc. With left needle tip, lift strand between needles from back to front. Knit lifted loop through front of loop	**rem**	remain(ing)	**tog**	together
				rep(s)	repeat(s)	**tr**	treble crochet (US double crochet)
DK	double knitting			**rev st st**	reverse stocking stitch		
DPN	double-pointed needle						
est	established			**RH**	right hand	**w&t**	wrap and turn
foll	following			**RS**	right side	**WS**	wrong side
inc	increase			**skpo**	slip 1 stitch, knit 1 stitch, pass slipped stitch over	**wyib**	with yarn in back
K	knit	**MB**	make a bobble			**wyif**	with yarn in front
KFB	knit into front and back of stitch	**MS**	main shade			**yb**	take yarn back (no inc)
		P	purl	**SI**	slip		
K2tog	knit the next two stitches together	**patt**	pattern(s)	**ss**	slip stitch (crochet)	**yfwd**	yarn forward
		PB	place bead	**slm**	slip marker	**yo**	yarn over
LH	left hand	**PFB**	purl into front and back of stitch	**SSK**	slip 2 sts one at a time, knit 2 slipped sts together tbl	**yrn**	yarn round needle
meas	measures						

Crochet Guide

Crochet techniques are often used in lace knitting to add a neat edge – follow our simple guide to the basics

CHAIN STITCH This is the foundation of all crochet stitches and can be used to make fancy edges

1 With the hook in your right hand, hold the yarn end in your right hand as well to provide tension. Hold the working yarn in your left hand. Move the hook under and over the yarn to wrap it around counter-clockwise.

2 Pull the hook towards the slip knot, catching the strand of yarn in the hook and pulling it through the slip knot loop. This forms your first chain (ch) stitch. Now repeat steps 1 and 2 to form a chain.

3 This is what your row of chains will look like. Hold the chain with your right hand near the hook, to keep the tension. Keep on going until you have the number of chains stated on your pattern.

SLIP STITCH Use this to neaten up your work and much more

1 Insert the hook from front to back into the second chain from the hook. When working into a chain, insert the hook into the center (two chain loops over the hook). Wrap yarn round the hook (yrh).

2 Pull the yarn through both loops of the chain stitch and the loop already on the hook to make a slip stitch. To carry on working a row of slip stitches, insert the hook into the next chain down and so on.

SINGLE CROCHET One of the key stitches in crochet, singles are simple, compact stitches that form a firm, neat edging

1 To make a single crochet stitch, insert the hook under the top two loops of the first stitch on the previous row.

2 Wind the yarn around the hook and pull it through the stitch, leaving two loops on your crochet hook.

3 Wind the yarn around hook again, then pull the yarn through both loops. There's your single crochet made and you'll have one loop left on your hook ready to do the next stitch. Continue to the end of the row.

4 For foll rows, turn and make 1 turning chain (t-ch). For sc only, this usually does not count as a st. Work the first sc of the row in the st at the base of the ch. At the end of the row, do not work in the top of the t-ch.

CREATING PERFECT LACE

Flawless lacework is achievable, if you follow Jane Crowfoot's expert tips on avoiding and correcting mistakes

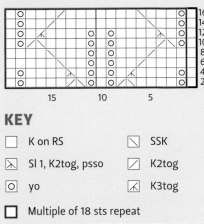

CHART

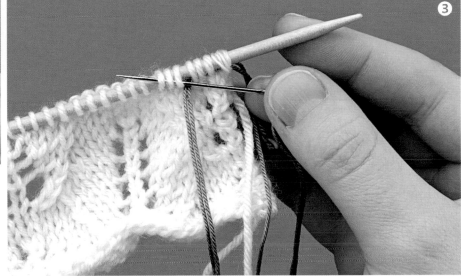

KEY

☐	K on RS	⧄	SSK
⋏	Sl 1, K2tog, psso	⁄	K2tog
○	yo	⋌	K3tog
☐	Multiple of 18 sts repeat		

Knitting lace patterns can require complete concentration and many hours of work. However, many knitters enjoy such a challenge – the production of a perfect piece of fine knitted lace seems to generate universal feelings of awe and pride among us knitters.

The complexity and labor-intensive nature of lace patterns mean it's all too easy to make mistakes, and this can be off-putting to those embarking upon their first lace project. However, there are some really useful tips that can help you to produce that elusive piece of perfect lace.

In this feature, we're going to take a look at some easy ways to avoid making mistakes in the first place, then explore the techniques you can use, should the worst happen.

If you're new to lace knitting, we'd recommend starting with a small project that has lace patterning on alternate rows. This type of project is referred to as *lace knitting*, as opposed to *knitted lace* which has lace patterning on all rows.

About our expert
Jane Crowfoot is one of the UK's leading knitting experts and author of the book *Finishing Techniques for Hand Knitters*

CHOOSING THE RIGHT PATTERN AND YARN
When choosing your first lace pattern, look for a relatively small project that will enable you to try different stitches without being overwhelming, such as the Marianne Purse (page 50). It's also worth trying to avoid yarns that are hard to unravel and dark-colored yarns, which can make the stitches hard to see.

READING CHARTS
The majority of lace patterns are now presented in chart form. Each instruction is represented by a symbol within the chart. These symbols are designed to show how they look in the knitted fabric.

Yarn-overs, for example, will appear as holes in the knitted fabric and are shown as circles on a chart. Right-leaning decreases (K2tog on RS) are shown as right-leaning slashes.

❶ Compare the sample above with its chart to see how the two relate to each other. Because this sample is lace knitting, the chart shows only RS rows, and WS rows are purled.

AVOIDING MISTAKES
It is common to make mistakes when working early repeats of a lace pattern. Once you have done a few repeats, the pattern will become easier to memorize, and you'll be able to recognize where you are. However, taking a few preventative measures can save lots of time.

Chart copy, sticky notes and markers
You can make a working copy of the chart, for your own personal use. Enlarging it will make it easier to read, and you can keep notes on the back of it as well.

Sticky notes are a really great way of keeping track of where you are in your pattern. Use them to block out the rows above, so you can see how the row you are working lines up with your knitting. ▶

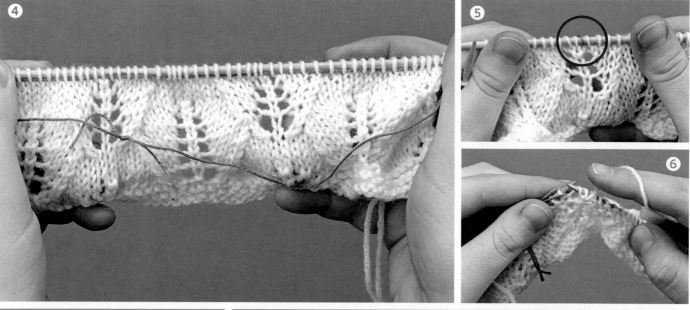

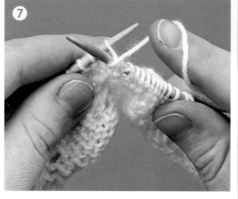

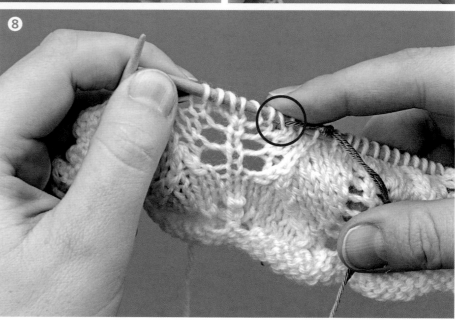

Stitch markers are useful when placed after each repeat of the stitch pattern in the row, to help you keep track of where you are in the pattern. Purpose-made markers are available, or you could simply use a knotted loop of mercerized cotton.

Using a life-line

A 'life-line' is a piece of cotton yarn threaded through a knitted row at the end of the pattern repeat. If a mistake is subsequently made, then the knitting can be unravelled back to the life-line and no further.

Life-lines can be used after each pattern repeat, or at the halfway point. In really complicated lace patterns, you may want to insert a life-line every couple of rows.

Step by step

❷ Use a large sewing needle with a blunt point and a smooth contrasting thread. Make sure the thread is long enough to leave you with ample yarn once sewn through the row. Mercerized cotton is perfect because it won't stick to the working yarn.

❸ Bring your needle and thread through the center of each stitch on the knitting needle, being careful not to sew through any stitch markers. If there isn't enough space to do this on the needle, slip the stitches off onto the sewing thread, and then slide the needle back in, once all stitches are on the life-line.

❹ Make sure that the life-line thread cannot loosen or unravel itself from the

row. Perhaps use safety pins to secure it at each tail end, or tie the ends in a knot.

FIXING MISTAKES

Of course, however prepared and careful you are, it's inevitable that mistakes will slip in. It's a good idea to check your work regularly – try to make a habit of counting stitches after most rows.

The following examples are based on the Hexagon Fern stitch pattern in the chart.

Correcting an error made on the previous row

If you make a mistake one row down, you could undo the row you've just knitted, but there are a few time-saving alternative fixes you could also try. Once you've

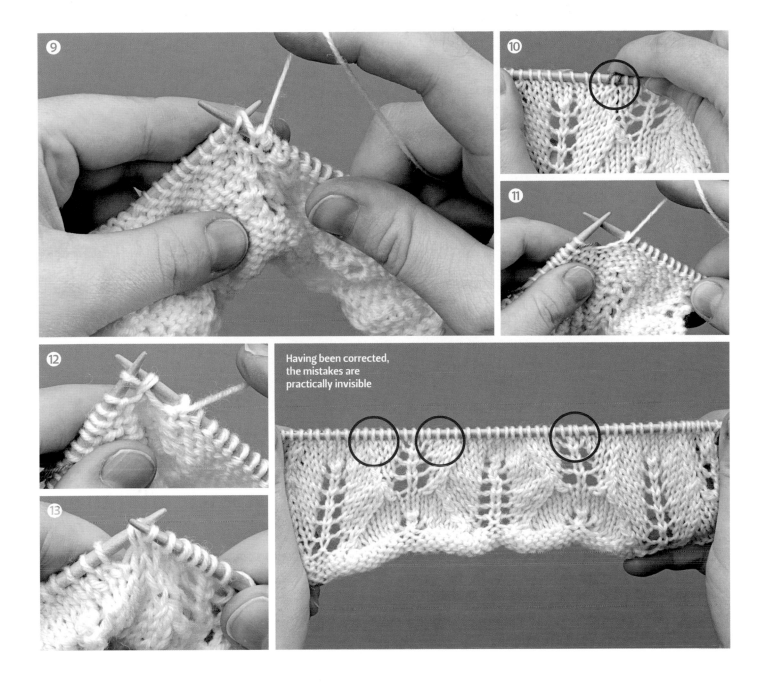

Having been corrected, the mistakes are practically invisible

identified the mistake, use a stitch marker to indicate its position and work along the row to that point.

Correcting a missed yarn-over

❺ This is one of the most common errors made in lace. In the sample on page 14, there should be a yarn-over on both sides of the central stitch (9 on the chart).

❻ Pick up the thread that runs between the two stitches where the yarn-over should have been made.

❼ Place this thread on the left-hand needle and treat it as if it is the next stitch in the pattern. This will make a slightly smaller hole than the others on the row, but once it has been blocked and pressed, it will not be noticeable.

Getting rid of an extra yarn-over

❽ The sample on page 14 has an extra yarn-over, which will make a hole in your fabric where you don't want it, and create an extra stitch.

❾ To get rid of the yarn-over, work up to it, then knit or purl it (depending upon which row you are on) together with the next stitch along. This will leave a very small hole, which won't be too obvious once the piece is blocked.

Correcting a decrease that leans in the wrong direction

❿ In the sample above, what should be a left-leaning decrease (SSK) has been wrongly worked as a right-leaning (K2tog) decrease.

⓫ To correct it, work along the row according to the pattern until you reach the mistake.

⓬ Insert the right-hand needle from the reverse to the front of each stitch at the same time and then allow the stitch above to unravel by dropping it from the left needle.

⓭ Rework the stitch in the correct way using the unravelled yarn.

Correcting an error made a few rows down

Although sometimes it is easiest to just unravel back to a life-line, a mistake made a few rows down can be fixed by just dropping a few stitches. The stitches can then be picked up again correctly, saving you from lots of re-knitting. ✥

GET THE PERFECT FINISH

Make your finished lace projects look as beautiful as possible. **Jane Crowfoot** explains how

Essential equipment for blocking lace includes pins or blocking wires, a ruler, a blocking board and a mild detergent

'Blocking' is the term used to describe the washing/wetting, laying out and steaming/drying of knitted pieces before they are sewn together. The process evens out the stitches and makes pieces far easier to put together because the seams are less prone to curling.

People block in many different ways, but there are some crucial things to remember and take into consideration. First, if your piece of lace has cast-on and cast-off edges, always make sure this is done loosely. Second, never be tempted to hurry – you should always take plenty of time for the 'finishing' process. In all cases, avoid placing a hot iron directly onto the knitted fabric because it can cause irreparable damage, especially to synthetic or manmade fibers.

Do not press ribs, cables, lace and textural stitches. Finally, always read the yarn ball band for washing and finishing instructions.

About the expert
Jane Crowfoot is one of the UK's leading knitting experts and author of the book *Finishing Techniques for Hand Knitters*

Blocking lace

Knitting lace can be very time-consuming, especially if you are making a large and beautiful piece, such as one of our lace shawls – Judy Furlong's Rose Shetland Shawl on page 36, for example, or Anniken Allis's Setting Sun Shawl on page 90. These involve working hundreds of stitches and rows in a very fine yarn. The key to really beautiful lace work lies in correct blocking.

It is only once blocked that lace work realizes its full beauty. The intricate stitching becomes more apparent, the stitches become 'set' in their stretched position and the knitted piece can grow considerably. Having spent so long on a piece, it would be a shame to rush the finish, so take your time and adhere to the following steps to ensure the perfect finish.

FIRST STEPS

Before you start the blocking process, make sure you have all the correct equipment to hand.
Blocking board: If you have plenty of room for storage, the ideal surface to work on is a blocking board. You can make your own board by placing a thin sheet of wadding between a piece of hardboard and some checked or gingham-type fabric. Stretch the fabric tightly and fix in place with staples or tape at the back. Some people prefer to use a large bathroom towel pinned to the floor, or a blanket covered with cotton fabric such as a bed sheet.

Whatever your preference, bear in mind that the piece needs to be left in place until it is dry, which could take a while.
Mild detergent: The most common outcome of poor care when washing a knitted fabric is felting. This is caused by friction, agitation and heat, or a combination of these.

Different types of yarn require different kinds of care, but the same principles for washing apply to most. Do not use biological washing powder or those with any kind of added 'brighteners'. Soap flakes, mild detergent and specially formulated liquids, such as Soak, are usually best. If in doubt, test a detergent on a gauge swatch before use on the finished item. Make sure the water is cool and the detergent is completely dissolved. If the detergent needs warm or hot water in order to disperse thoroughly, make sure it has had time to cool before washing. ▶

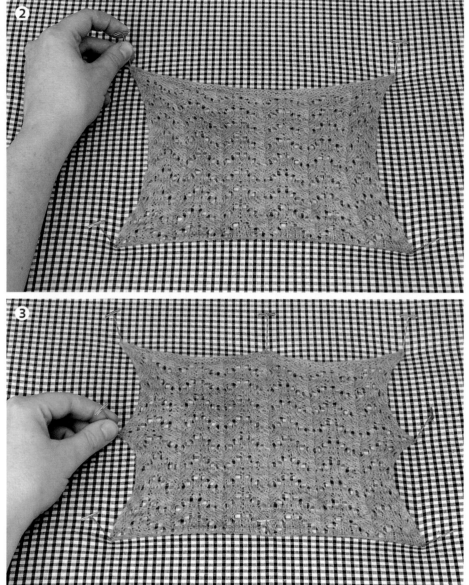

Be careful not to use too much detergent – a small dribble of liquid should suffice.

Clean, thick bath towels: These are used to remove excess water from the knitted fabric. Be careful if using brand new towels as these can often be 'slippery' and can shed their own fiber.

Pins: Quilters' T-pins are really good for blocking. However, most pins are suitable, but the longer they are, the better. Make sure that the pins you use are rust-proof and easy to handle, and that you have plenty of them! You'll generally need more than you think.

Blocking wires: Blocking wires are a very handy blocking buddy, if not an essential part of your kit. You can often buy them in packs of four or eight, and they are available in varying lengths. Wires are particularly handy when blocking regular shapes such as squares, triangles and rectangles, but are not used when blocking half or full circles. The use of blocking wires will mean that you require fewer pins for blocking. You could also try using welding wires, which are available from suppliers such as *www.thewelderswarehouse.com* and are often cheaper, though you may have to buy in bulk.

In place of blocking wires, you can opt to use a cotton thread, such as a fine yet strong crochet thread. A long length of thread can be sewn through the perimeter stitches of the knitted lace, leaving a loop at each corner. Place a pin into each corner loop and arrange the knitting along the taut string, pinning in pairs as you go.

Ruler or set square: A ruler of some kind will help you to ensure that you have blocked your piece straight and evenly.

WASHING

❶ Always wash one piece at a time. Do not wring, twist or rub the fabric, and never use a brush to remove spots or stains. You will need to leave the piece to soak for a minimum of 15 minutes to ensure that the yarn has absorbed its optimum amount of water. Some yarns (cotton and linen especially) can take surprisingly long to soak fully.

Always make sure the water runs clear after the final rinse.

Remove as much water as you can by pushing the knitted piece gently against the side of the basin or bowl in which you have washed it.

When you've managed to remove a fair amount of water, you will need to transfer the piece onto a clean towel. It is vital that you support the piece in its transition from basin to towel. By placing the piece in a colander – check it has no rough edges – you will support the fabric fully and avoid excess stretching and pulling.

Place your knitted piece between two clean, thick bath towels and carefully press to remove excess water. You need to remove as much water as possible in this process. Some people roll the knitting up in the towel and push against it. Others lay the piece out flat between the two towels and carefully walk on it or add weight of some kind.

PINNING OUT

Gently pin out your knitted piece onto your chosen blocking surface.

❷ For a geometric shape such as a triangle, square or rectangle, pin out the corners first, followed by the top middle point, then the corresponding point opposite this on the bottom edge,

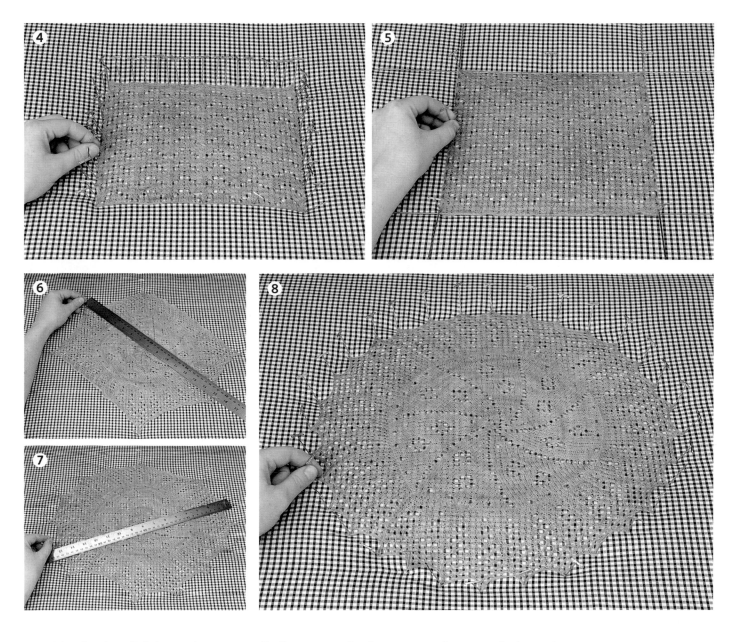

stretching the piece slightly in order to achieve its true length.

❸ Always place the pins into your fabric in pairs from the center out, making sure that for every pin you place in one edge, you also put in its 'partner' along the opposite edge.

❹ This will ensure that you pin out your knitting evenly. Use your ruler to ensure that you are pinning in a straight line (this is where a gingham or checked blocking board cover comes in handy, as you can pin along the fabric lines).

❺ For geometric shapes you can replace some of the pins with dressing wires. These are carefully threaded through the edge stitches of the knitted fabric. Use your fingers to ease along the edges so that the lace is fully stretched out. Place pins at each corner and a couple of places along the edges to secure the lace.

❻+❼ For a circular shape, pin out the four compass points, then work around the piece, placing pins in pairs as for a geometric shape.

❽ To ensure you block your knitting into a true circle, you may want to work on top of an image. To do this, draw a circle using a fine pencil or dressmaker's chalk onto the blocking board and then pin out your knitting to the drawn line.

LET IT DRY

The impatient among you will have to take yourself out for the day or settle down to knit your next project in front of a few good movies before the piece is dry. Do not be tempted to unpin your piece until you are convinced it is thoroughly dry. You may find that the piece has raised itself away from the blocking board slightly and has gone pretty taut – a little like the skin

of a drum. This is caused by the yarn retracting and shrinking slightly as it dries. The drying time will depend on the climate, but the general rule of thumb is to wait 24 hours. Just remember that the wait is worth it! Also, remember that the blocking process will need to be repeated every time the lace piece is washed. ☻

Samples knitted in The Knitting Goddess 100% Cashmere Lace weight.

Top ten...
Tips for washing

It's worth investing a little time to look after your precious handknits by washing them carefully...

1 Check the label
Unfortunately, hand-knitted items don't come with a label, so check the yarn's ball band for washing advice, and keep ball bands safe so you can refer to them before washing.

2 Test swatches
If you're in the good habit of making swatches, put them to good use by using them in a test wash. Note the measurements of your swatch and then wash it, following the advice below, to see whether the size, shape, color and texture change.

3 Hand or machine?
Treat hand-knits with respect and wash by hand. Some ball bands say that machine-washing is possible, but we recommend you test this with a swatch first. You'll usually need the gentlest, coolest wool setting; follow the advice below.

4 The right detergent
Gentle is the key word when washing hand-knits so use just a little gentle detergent. Some knitters use a basic or eco-friendly washing liquid.

5 Warm not hot
Knits need water that's not too hot, to avoid felting and pilling. Aim for lukewarm water that feels like the same temperature as your hand.

6 Offer support
Fibers are vulnerable when wet, so never rub or squeeze! If you need to, gently press against the side of the bowl. When removing from the water, support its weight with a hand underneath.

7 Rinse well
Most detergents need rinsing several times, in gradually colder water that won't shock the fibers. In the final rinse, some knitters use a spoonful of fabric softener or white vinegar, but test this on your swatch first.

8 Color issues
Color bleeding is always a risk and a small amount is natural. If your item leaks a lot of color, rinse quickly in cold water and remove the water as fast as you can. For hand-dyed yarns, check the dyer's advice before washing.

9 In a spin
After rinsing, never wring! Instead, place the item between two towels, roll up and press gently. Some knitters spin items in the washing machine, on the slowest setting, for 10 seconds to a minute. For small items, try a salad spinner.

10 Drying time
Lay your item out flat on dry towels – never hang it up. Gently reshape it, fasten any buttons and leave to air dry, avoiding direct sunlight. If this is the item's first wash, you may need to block with pins. Drying can take up to three days, so change the towels regularly. ⊕

THE JAN
SWEATER

All-seasons lace

COCKLESHELL
LACE TOP

LAZULI
SHAWL

ENCHANTED
SHRUG

ROSE
SHETLAND
SHAWL

Amanda Jones

Cockleshell Lace Top

A feminine top that is interesting to knit,
in an affordable yarn that drapes beautifully

SIZE

		10-12	14	16-18	20-22	
TO FIT BUST		90	96	104	114	cm
		35½	38	41	45	in
LENGTH TO SHOULDER		55	56	57	58	cm
		21¾	22	22½	23	in
SLEEVE LENGTH (UNDERARM TO WRIST)		32	32	32	32	cm
		12½	12½	12½	12½	in

YARN

This project was stitched with **Sirdar** Snuggly Baby Bamboo, DK (US: sport weight), in Tulip (136) (80% bamboo, 20% wool), 1¾oz/50g, 104yds/95m

TULIP	7	8	9	10	x 50g BALLS

Unfortunately, this color is now discontinued, but there are plenty of other shades available including two pinks, FlipFlop (125) and Babe (134).

NEEDLES

1 pair of 4mm (UK 8/US 6) needles
2.5mm (size 12) crochet hook

GAUGE

23 sts and 26 rows to 4in (10cm) worked over stocking st on 4mm needles

ABBREVIATIONS

yrn: yarn round needle. Between two purl sts, take yarn back over right needle and forward under right needle.
DC: double crochet (see page 11 for explanation).
SS: slip st crochet (see page 11 for explanation).

Amanda Jones
Cockleshell Lace Top

DELICATE SHELL PATTERNS and a scalloped hem give a real seaside flavor to this lacy top from Amanda Jones.

Sirdar Snuggly Baby Bamboo yarn is ideal for garments in all seasons, thanks to the cool bamboo and touch of woolen warmth. It's light, soft and drapes beautifully when knitted up.

The lacy shell stitch pattern on this top is produced by knitting a series of yarnovers to give holes in a leaf-like arrangement. Loops of yarn are then drawn through the holes in order, from right to left, and then knitted together on the following row. Simple shells!

BACK

Using 4mm needles cast on 101 (111:121:131) sts.
Row 1 (RS): *K1, bring yarn to front, K3, sl1, K2tog, psso, K3, bring yarn to front; rep from * to last st, K1.
Row 2: P.
Rep these 2 rows, 2 more times. These 6 rows are shown on Chart A.

The next 10 rows form the border patt, which is also shown in Chart B (where the decrease row is not shown).
Row 7 (RS): *K3, K2tog, bring yarn to front, K1, bring yarn to front, K2tog tbl, K2; rep from * to last st, K1.
Row 8 and foll even rows: P.
Row 9: *K2, K2tog, bring yarn to front, K3, bring yarn to front, K2tog tbl, K1; rep from * to last st, K1.
Row 11: *K1, K2tog, bring yarn to front,

K5, bring yarn to front, K2tog tbl; rep from * to last st, K1.
Row 13 (decrease row): K2tog tbl, K to last 2 sts, K2tog.
99 (109:119:129) sts.
Row 15: K4, *insert right-hand needle in furthest right hole in Row 11, bring yarn to front and draw through to make a long loop which is kept on needle; rep from * into each of the remaining 5 spaces of leaf from right to left, K5, **K5, *insert right-hand needle in furthest right hole in Row 11, bring yarn to front and draw through to make a long loop which is kept on needle; rep from * into each of the remaining 5 spaces of leaf from right to left, K5; rep from ** to end.
Row 16 (WS): *P4, purl tog the 6 long loops with the next st, P5; rep from* to last 9 sts (and 6 loops), P4, purl tog the 6 long loops with the next st, P4.

The next rows set main pattern. Work as established, decreasing one st at each end of row 3 and every following 6th row until there are 91 (101:111:121) sts. Decreased sts are taken out of stockinette stitch edges, and are not shown below.

Row 1 (RS): K10 (5:10:15), Chart C row 1, K0 (5:5:5), Chart D row 1, K1 (6:6:6), Chart C row 1, K0 (5:5:5), Chart D row 1, K1 (6:6:6), Chart C row 1, K10 (5:10:15).
Row 2: P.
Row 3: K10 (5:10:15), Chart C row 3,

CHART A
Rows 1-6, patt rpt 10 sts + 1

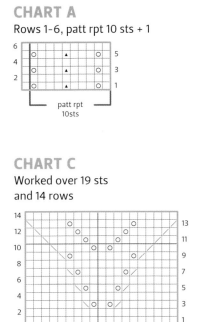

patt rpt
10sts

CHART B
Border pattern, rows 7-16, patt rpt 10 sts + 1

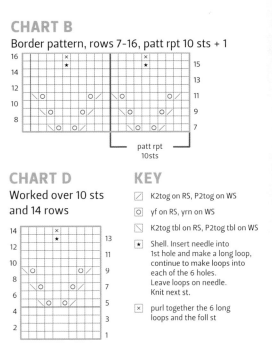

patt rpt
10sts

BLOCKING DIAGRAMS

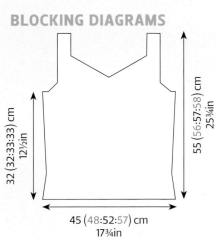

32 (32:33:33) cm
12½in

55 (56:57:58) cm
25¾in

45 (48:52:57) cm
17¾in

CHART C
Worked over 19 sts
and 14 rows

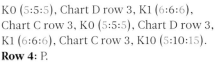

CHART D
Worked over 10 sts
and 14 rows

KEY

- ⊘ K2tog on RS, P2tog on WS
- ⊙ yf on RS, yrn on WS
- ⊠ K2tog tbl on RS, P2tog tbl on WS
- ★ Shell. Insert needle into 1st hole and make a long loop, continue to make loops into each of the 6 holes. Leave loops on needle. Knit next st.
- ⊠ purl together the 6 long loops and the foll st

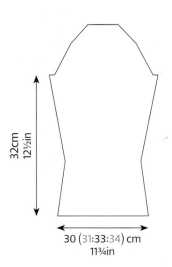

32cm
12½in

30 (31:33:34) cm
11¾in

K0 (5:5:5), Chart D row 3, K1 (6:6:6), Chart C row 3, K0 (5:5:5), Chart D row 3, K1 (6:6:6), Chart C row 3, K10 (5:10:15).
Row 4: P.
Row 5: K10 (5:10:15), Chart C row 5, K0 (5:5:5), Chart D row 5, K1 (6:6:6), Chart C row 5, K0 (5:5:5), Chart D row 5, K1 (6:6:6), Chart C row 5, K10 (5:10:15).
Row 6: P.
Row 7: K10 (5:10:15), Chart C row 7, K0 (5:5:5), Chart D row 7, K1 (6:6:6), Chart C row 7, K0 (5:5:5), Chart D row 7, K1 (6:6:6), Chart C row 7, K10 (5:10:15).
Rows 8 to 14 as established.

Once decreasing is complete and you have 91(101:111:121) sts, work straight for a further 8 rows.
Then, inc 1 st at both ends of the next and every foll 0 (6th:8th:8th) row until there are 93 (113:121:131) sts.
Cont working straight until the work measures 32 (32:33:33) cm (12 ½ [12½:13:13] in) from beg, ending on a WS row (5 full patt reps plus 0 [0:4:4] rows).

ARMHOLE SHAPING
(RS) Cast off 4 (4:4:5) sts at the beg of the next 2 rows. 85(105:113:121) sts. Then dec 1 st at each end of the next 3 (3:3:5) rows then on the foll 3(2:3:3) alt rows. 73 (95:101:105) sts.

Sizes 10 to 14 only
Because of the shaping and decreased

number of sts, the first and last repeats of Chart C must be modified. Keep center sts of pattern lined up as established. Cont to work the center repeats as before.

Modified Chart C for side repeats:
Rows 1 to 9: Work as before, with fewer stockinette stitch stitches before motif as appropriate.
Row 10 (WS): As Chart C row 3.
Row 11 (RS): As Chart C row 5.
Row 12: As Chart C row 7.
Row 13: As Chart C row 9.
Cont working until the armhole measures 16½cm (6½in) from beg of shaping ending on a WS row (3 full patt reps plus 2 rows).

Sizes 16 to 22 only
Continue to work in full pattern as established, until armhole measures 16½cm (6½in) from beg of shaping, ending with a WS row (3 full patt repeats plus 2 rows).

BACK NECK SHAPING (ALL SIZES)
Keeping patt correct, work across 22 (28:29:30) sts. Turn, leave rem sts on a spare needle and cont to work each side separately.
Dec 1 st at neck edge on every row until 17(19:21:25) sts rem.
Complete last patt plus 1 WS row. Cast off.
With RS facing rejoin yarn and cast off center 29 (39:43:45) sts, patt to end of row. Complete to match the first side. ▶

The border motif features an unusual shell stitch that inspired the pattern's name

The cockleshell motif runs around the borders and up the front and back of the top

FRONT

Work front of garment as for the back until you have completed 1 full patt rep after the beg of the armhole shaping, plus 2 rows.

FRONT NECK SHAPING

Keeping the patt correct work across 36 (47:50:52) sts, turn and leave rem sts on a spare needle. Work each side separately. Dec 1 st at the neck edge until 17 (19:21:25) sts rem. Cont working without shaping until the front matches to the back shoulder. Cast off.
With RS facing, rejoin yarn to other side of front and cast off 1 st. Patt to end of row. Complete to match the first side.

SLEEVES (work two alike)

Using 4mm needles cast on 61 (61:71:71) sts and work rows 1 to 16 as given for the back.
Dec 1 st at each end of the 13th and every foll 4th (6th:4th:6th) row, keeping patt correct, until 51 (57:61:65) sts remain. When you have completed all 16 rows of the border patt cont in main patt as folls:
Row 1 (RS): K.
Row 2: P.
Row 3: K19 (19:24:24), Chart C row 3, K19 (19:24:24).
Row 4: P.
This sets up the position for Chart C; cont working as described for back pattern. At the same time, dec 1 st at each end of every 4th (6th:4th:6th) row until 51(57:61:65) sts rem.

Work 8 (20:8:8) rows, then inc 1 st at both ends of the next row, then on the foll 6th (6th:6th:6th), then on the foll 4th (-:-: 4th). Cont to inc in this way until there are 69 (71:77:83) sts. Cont without shaping until you have completed 5 full patt reps, thus ending on a WS row.

SHAPE SLEEVE HEAD

Cast off 4 (4:4:5) sts at beg of the next 2 rows.
61(63:69:73) sts.

Dec 1 st at both ends of next 5 rows, then on the foll 5(5:6:6) alt rows. 41 (43:47:51) sts.
Dec 1 st at both ends of every foll 4th row until 33 (35:37:37) sts rem, then on every foll alt row until 27 (29:33:33) sts rem.
Dec 1 st at both ends of every foll row until 17 (19:21:21)sts rem.
Cast off rem sts.

FINISHING

Join shoulder seams.
Being careful to match patterns, join the side seams.
Join the sleeve seam.
Matching the center of the sleeve seam to the shoulder seam, set in the sleeves.

NECK BAND

Using 2.5mm crochet hook, with RS facing, starting at the left front shoulder, working in DC, work to center front. Work a SS into the center st, then cont in DC all around the neck.
Work 1 row of SS all around neck.
Block top out carefully to the measurements given in the schematics. ✪

Anniken Allis

Lazuli Shawl

Delicate stitch pattern stands out
beautifully in a bright lace weight yarn

Anniken Allis

Lazuli Shawl

SIZE

Width (wingspan): 84½in (214cm)
after blocking
Length (along spine): 45¼in (115cm)
after blocking

YARN

This project was stitched with **Yarn Addict**
Amazing Cashmere Lace, lace weight, in
Peacock (100% cashmere); 1¾oz/50g,
437yds/400m. Use 2 x 50g skeins.

Unfortunately this yarn is now discontinued,
but you can use any lace weight yarn that's
800m to 100g.

NEEDLES & ACCESSORIES

1 set 3.75mm (UK 9/US 5) circular needles,
approx 39in (100cm) long
Stitch markers

GAUGE

16 sts and 24 rows over main lace pattern
should measure 3½x3½in (9x9cm)
after blocking.

SPECIAL ABBREVIATIONS

sk2po: Sl 1, K2tog, psso. 2 sts decreased.

Delicate fir cone
stitch pattern is
easy to work

THE ONLINE yarn shop Yarn Addict
specializes in luxury yarns hand-dyed
by Anniken Allis. She is also a brilliant
designer, and her Lazuli lace shawl is the
perfect pattern for showing off your
favorite lace weight yarn. Though the
original yarn has been discontinued,
Anniken has a gorgeous range so you're
bound to find a great substitute.

This pattern is given in both written
and charted form. Written instructions
are given first, but if you prefer to use
charts, you will find these instructions
opposite. Though approximate gauge is
given, it is not essential.

SHAWL

Cast on 7 sts.

SET-UP PATTERN

Row 1 (RS): K2, *yo, K1, yo*, K1, rep from
* to *, K2. 11 sts.
Row 2 & all foll WS rows: K2, purl to last
2 sts, K2.
Row 3: K2, *yo, K3, yo,* K1, rep from * to *,
K2. 15 sts.
Row 5: K2, *yo, K5, yo,* K1, rep from * to *,
K2. 19 sts.
Row 7: K2, *yo, K7, yo,* K1, rep from * to *,
K2. 23 sts.
Row 9: K2, *yo, K1, yo, K2, sk2po, K2, yo,
K1, yo,* K1, rep from * to *, K2. 27 sts.
Row 11: K2, *yo, K2, yo, K2, sk2po, K2, yo,

K2, yo,* K1, rep from * to *, K2. 31 sts.
Row 13: K2, *yo, K3, yo, K2, sk2po, K2, yo,
K3, yo,* K1, rep from * to *, K2. 35 sts.
Row 15: K2, *yo, K4, yo, K2, sk2po, K2, yo,
K4, yo,* K1, rep from * to *, K2. 39 sts.
Row 17: K2, *yo, K1, yo, K2, sk2po, K2, yo,
K1, yo, K2, sk2po, K2, yo, K1, yo,* K1,
rep from * to *, K2. 43 sts.
Row 19: K2, *yo, K2, yo, K2, sk2po, K2, yo,
K1, yo, K2, sk2po, K2, yo, K2, yo,* K1,
rep from * to *, K2. 47 sts.
Row 21: K2, *yo, K3, yo, K2, sk2po, K2, yo,
K1, yo, K2, sk2po, K2, yo, K3, yo,* K1,
rep from * to *, K2. 51 sts.
Row 23: K2, *yo, K4, yo, K2, sk2po, K2, yo,
K1, yo, K2, sk2po, K2, yo, K4, yo,* K1,
rep from * to *, K2. 55 sts.

MAIN PATTERN

Row 1 (RS): K2, *yo, K1, yo, K2, sk2po, K2,
yo, (K1, yo, K2, sk2po, K2, yo), K1, yo, K2,
sk2po, K2, yo, K1, yo,* K1, rep from * to *,
K2.
Row 2 & all foll WS rows: K2, purl to last
2 sts, K2.
Row 3: K2, *yo, K2, yo, K2, sk2po, K2, yo,
(K1, yo, K2, sk2po, K2, yo), K1, yo, K2,
sk2po, K2, yo, K2, yo,* K1, rep from * to *,
K2.
Row 5: K2, *yo, K3, yo, K2, sk2po, K2, yo,
(K1, yo, K2, sk2po, K2, yo), K1, yo, K2,
sk2po, K2, yo, K3, yo,* K1, rep from * to *,
K2.
Row 7: K2, *yo, K4, yo, K2, sk2po, K2, yo,

(K1, yo, K2, sk2po, K2, yo), K1, yo, K2,
sk2po, K2, yo, K4, yo,* K1, rep from * to *,
K2. 71 sts.
Row 8 (WS): K2, purl to last 2 sts, K2.
These 8 rows set pattern.

Stitch counts inc by 16 sts for each 8-row
repeat. The section marked in brackets is
repeated one more time after each 8-row
repeat. Work a total of 184 rows in main
pattern (22 more reps). After all 23 repeats
are complete, you should have 423 sts.

BORDER PATTERN

Row 1 (RS): K2, *yo, K1, yo, K2, sk2po, K2,
yo, (K1, yo, K2, sk2po, K2, yo) 24 times, K1,
yo, K2, sk2po, K2, yo, K1, yo,* K1, rep from
* to *, K2. 427 sts.
Row 2 & all foll WS rows: K2, purl to last
2 sts, K2.
Row 3: K2, *yo, K3, yo, K1, sk2po, K1, yo,
K1, (K2, yo, K1, sk2po, K1, yo, K1) 24 times,
K2, yo, K1, sk2po, K1, yo, K3, yo,* K1,
rep from * to *, K2. 431 sts.
Row 5: K2, *yo, K5, yo, sk2po, yo, K2, (K3,
yo, sk2po, yo, K2) 24 times, K3, yo, sk2po,
yo, K5, yo,* K1, rep from * to *, K2. 435 sts.
Row 7: K2, *yo, K6, yo, sk2po, yo, K2, (K3,
yo, sk2po, yo, K2) 24 times, K3, yo, sk2po,
yo, K6, yo,* K1, rep from * to *, K2. 439 sts.
Row 9: K2, *yo, K7, yo, sk2po, yo, K2, (K3,
yo, sk2po, yo, K2) 24 times, K3, yo, sk2po,
yo, K7, yo,* K1, rep from * to *, K2. 443 sts.
Row 11: K2, *yo, K8, yo, sk2po, yo, K2, (K3,

CHARTS

MAIN CHART

Only RS rows are charted. Purl WS rows.

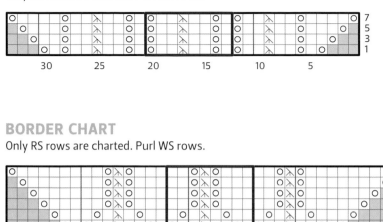

BORDER CHART

Only RS rows are charted. Purl WS rows.

SET-UP CHART

Only RS rows are charted. Purl WS rows.

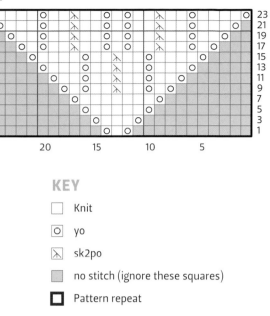

KEY

☐	Knit
⊡	yo
⋏	sk2po
▨	no stitch (ignore these squares)
☐	Pattern repeat

Putting a stitch marker on each side of the central stitch helps to keep the pattern correct

yo, sk2po, yo, K2) 24 times, K3, yo, sk2po, yo, K8, yo,* K1, rep from * to *, K2. 447 sts.

Cast off all sts using Russian cast-off method, as follows:
K2, pass both sts back to left needle and K2tog, *K1, pass both sts back to left needle and K2tog; rep from * to end of row.

FINISHING

Soak shawl in tepid water for at least 20 minutes. Carefully squeeze water out, and then press between towels to remove excess water.
Pin shawl out to measurements using pins and wires, or just pins, to make straight edges and accentuate the scalloped bottom edge.
Leave until fully dry and unpin. Weave in all ends and trim.

SHAWL USING CHARTS

Cast on 7 sts.
Working all rows as set below, work from set-up chart once.
Work Main Chart 23 times.
Work Border Chart once.
RS rows: K2, work chart, K1, work chart, K2.
WS rows: K2, purl to last 2 sts, K2.
Cast off using Russian cast-off method (see above).

Work finishing instructions as above. ⊕

Susan Crawford

The Jan Sweater

1930s sweater uses bold lines of lace to create
a flattering fit for every vintage lover

The Jan Sweater

SIZE

	6-8	10-12	14-16	18-20	22-24	
TO FIT BUST	81	86-92	97-102	107-112	117-122	cm
	32	34-36	38-40	42-44	46-48	in
ACTUAL BUST	86	97	107	119	129	cm
	34	38	42	47	51	in
ACTUAL LENGTH	48	48	52	54½	58½	cm
	19	19	20½	21½	23	in

YARN

Excelana 4ply Luxury Wool (4ply weight; 100% pure new British wool; 159m/50g balls)

POWDERED EGG (08)	5	5	6	7	8	x50g BALLS

BLOCKING DIAGRAM

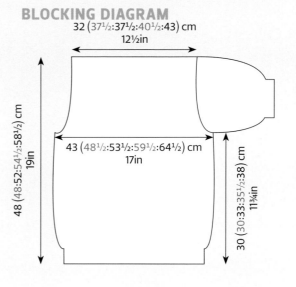

32 (37½:37½:40½:43) cm
12½in

48 (48:52:54½:58½) cm
19in

43 (48½:53½:59½:64½) cm
17in

30 (30:33:35½:38) cm
11¾in

THIS DAINTY little sweater is from the mid-1930s and is feminine and flattering. It has been updated by Susan Crawford to fit bust sizes from 32in to 48in.

Designed to be worn at the waist and with an attractive boat neckline, this garment is suitable for any occasion. Knit it in a 4ply wool, in a vintage shade of Powdered Egg, and you too can feel like a character in Agatha Christie's *Poirot*!

This garment is constructed in four separate pieces. It is designed with some wearing ease to allow the body to 'blouse' slightly over the ribbed welt.

BACK

Using 2.75mm needles cast on 86 (100:114:128:142) sts.
Next row: * K1, P1, rep from * to end.
Repeat this row until work meas 8½cm, ending with a WS row.

Next row (inc): Still working in rib, inc 25 sts evenly across the row.
111 (125:139:153:167) sts.

Change to 3.25mm needles and work in stitch pattern as folls:

Row 1 (WS): P.
Row 2: K.
Row 3: P.
Row 4: K6, * yo, K2tog, K5, repeat from * to end.
Row 5: P.
Row 6: K.
Row 7: P.
Row 8: K5, (yo, K2tog, K5) 7 (8:9:10:11) times, yo, K2tog, K1, (yo, K5, K2tog) 7 (8:9:10:11) times, yo, K5.
112 (126:140:154:168) sts.
Row 9: P.
Row 10: K.
Row 11: P.
Row 12: K4, (yo, K2tog, K5) 7 (8:9:10:11) times. yo, K2tog, K2, K2tog, (yo, K5, K2tog) 7 (8:9:10:11) times, yo, K4.
Row 13: P.
Row 14: K.
Row 15: P.
Row 16: K3, (yo, K2tog, K5) 7 (8:9:10:11) times. yo, K2tog, K4, K2tog, (yo, K5, K2tog) 7 (8:9:10:11) times, yo, K3.
Row 17: P.
Row 18: K.
Row 19: P.
Row 20: K2, (yo, K2tog, K5) 7 (8:9:10:11) times. yo, K2tog, K6, K2tog, (yo, K5, K2tog) 7 (8:9:10:11) times, yo, K2.
Row 21: P.
Row 22: K.

▶

NEEDLES

1 pair 2.75mm (UK 12/US 2) needles
1 pair 3.25mm (UK 10/US 3) needles

GAUGE

26 sts and 36 rows to 4in (10cm) using 3.25mm needles over stitch pattern
28 sts and 36 rows to 4in (10cm) using 3.25mm needles over st st

YARN DETAILS

Susan's vintage-style Excelana yarn can be ordered directly from her by visiting **www.susancrawfordvintage.com**. The 4ply weight is available in eight delicate and complementary shades.

© SUSAN CRAWFORD 2011

❝WITH AN ATTRACTIVE BOAT NECKLINE, THIS LACY TOP IS PERFECT FOR ANY OCCASION❞

In detail
Adapting your top

The neckline is not joined together except for where the sleevehead meets the body. If the wearer has narrow shoulders, the neck can be sewn together for about an inch to prevent the garment slipping off down the arms.

The simple lace 'V' pattern is worked with a center eyelet; the design then mirrors itself on either side of this center pattern repeat. The garment is easy to lengthen by working more repeats below the armhole shaping.

Row 23: P.
Row 24: K1, (yo, K2tog, K5) 7 (8:9:10:11) times, yo, K2tog, K8, K2tog, (yo, K5, K2tog) 7 (8:9:10:11) times, yo, K1.
Row 25: P.
Row 26: K.
Row 27: P.
Row 28: K7, (yo, K2tog, K5) 6 (7:8:9:10) times, yo, K2tog, K10, K2tog, (yo, K5, K2tog) 6 (7:8:9:10) times, yo, K7.
Row 29: P.
Row 30: K.
Row 31: P.
Row 32: K6, (yo, K2tog, K5) 7 (8:9:10:11) times, (K2tog, yo, K5) 8 (9:10:11:12) times, K1.
Row 33: P.
Row 34: K.
Row 35: P.
Row 36: K5, (yo, K2tog, K5) 7 (8:9:10:11) times, yo, K2tog, K2tog, (yo, K5, K2tog) 7 (8:9:10:11) times, yo, K5.

Repeat from row 9 until work meas 30½ (30½:33:35½:38) cm or desired length to underarm, ending with a WS row.

SHAPE ARMHOLE
Keeping pattern correct, cast off 7 sts at beginning of the next 2 (2:2:4:4) rows, then decrease 1 st at each end of every alt row 7 (7:14:11:14) times.
84 (98:98:104:112) sts.

Continue working in pattern until armhole meas 18 (18:19:19:20) cm from cast-off, ending with a WS row.

Next row (RS): * K1, P1, rep from * to end. Repeat this row until rib meas 2½cm.

© SUSAN CRAWFORD 2011

Cast off fairly loosely in rib.

FRONT
Work exactly as for Back.

SLEEVES
Using 2.75mm needles cast on 62 (62:76:90:104) sts.
Next row: * K1, P1, rep from * to end. Repeat this row until work meas 4cm, ending with a WS row.

Next row (inc): Still working in rib, inc 21 sts evenly across row.
83 (83:97:111:125) sts.

Change to 3.25mm needles and work in pattern as for Back until sleeve meas 13 (13:14:15:15) cm. 84 (84:98:112:126) sts.

SHAPE SLEEVEHEAD
Cast off 3 sts at the beginning of every row until 18 (18:20:28:30) sts rem.
Cast off rem sts.

FINISHING
Steam pieces on wrong side with a warm iron and a damp cloth. Join underarm seams.
Work tacking stitches across front and back shoulders to hold in place while attaching sleeves. Sew up sleeve seams and sew sleeves in place.
Darn in all ends. ✛

Grace Mcewen

Enchanted Shrug

Lacy leaves in subtle tones cascade gently
around the wearer of this delicate wrap

Grace Mcewen
Enchanted Shrug

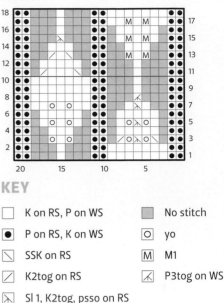

SIZE
51in (130cm) long by 15½in (40cm wide)

YARN
This project was stitched with **The Natural Dye Studio** Angel 2ply, lace weight (70% baby alpaca, 20% silk, 10% cashmere); 3 ½oz/100g, 875yds/800m
Aqua 1 x 100g skein
Aqua is unfortunately now sold out, but a range of other shades are available.

NEEDLES & ACCESSORIES
1 pair 4mm (UK 8/US 6) knitting needles
Stitch markers

GAUGE
14 sts and 18 rows of lace pattern over 2in by 2½in (5cm by 6½cm), relaxed after blocking

SPECIAL ABBREVIATIONS
sk2po: Slip 1 stitch, knit 2 stitches together, pass slipped stitch over

CHART

KEY

☐ K on RS, P on WS	▨ No stitch
● P on RS, K on WS	O yo
◻ SSK on RS	M M1
◻ K2tog on RS	◻ P3tog on WS
◻ Sl 1, K2tog, psso on RS	

DESIGNER GRACE MCEWEN was inspired by the view from her Massachusetts window when creating this lace pattern. She says: "In the breeze, the leaves take on a life of their own, dancing along elegantly. The leaves on this shrug gently cascade along the wearer, creating a gentle warmth. They travel in both directions and drape wonderfully."

The shrug is knitted in one long piece, then both outside sections are sewn up lengthways to create sleeves.

The scalloped edges of the piece draw attention to the lovely lace leaves. "When blocking, allow the leaves on the edges to flow and avoid trying to make the edges straight," Grace advises.

STITCH PATTERN
Worked over 14 sts and 18 rows. Stitch count changes during pattern, so check stitches are correct on row 1.
Row 1: *P2, K7, P2, K1, P2; rep from * to end.
Row 2: *K2, P1, K2, P7, K2; rep from * to end.
Row 3: *P2, SSK, yo, sk2po, yo, K2tog, P2, yo, K1, yo, P2; rep from * to end.
Row 4: *K2, P3, K2, P5, K2; rep from * to end.
Row 5: *P2, K1, yo, sk2po, yo, K1, P2, K1, yo, K1, yo, K1, P2; rep from * to end.
Row 6: *K2, P5, K2, P5, K2; rep from * to end.

Row 7: *P2, K1, sk2po, K1, P2, K2, yo, K1, yo, K2, P2; rep from * to end.
Row 8: *K2, P7, K2, P3tog, K2; rep from * to end.
Row 9: *P2, K1, P2, K7, P2; rep from * to end.
Row 10: *K2, P7, K2, P1, K2; rep from * to end.
Row 11: *P2, K1, P2, SSK, K3, K2tog, P2; rep from * to end.
Row 12: *K2, P5, K2, P1, K2; rep from * to end.
Row 13: *P2, M1, K1, M1, P2, SSK, K1, K2tog, P2; rep from * to end.
Row 14: *K2, P3, K2, P3, K2; rep from * to end.
Row 15: *P2, K1, M1, K1, M1, K1, P2, sk2po, P2; rep from * to end.
Row 16: *K2, P1, K2, P5, K2; rep from * to end.
Row 17: *P2, K2, M1, K1, M1, K2, P2, K1, P2; rep from * to end.
Row 18: *K2, P1, K2, P7, K2; rep from * to end.

SHRUG
Loosely cast on 112 stitches using 4mm straight needles.
Begin working stitch pattern, placing stitch markers every 14 stitches to mark repeats, if desired.

Continue working in stitch pattern for 20 complete repeats (360 rows in total). Cast off all stitches loosely. The sewn cast-off technique works well.

With only 14 stitches and 18 rows, this lace pattern is quick to master

FINISHING
Block the piece firmly to measurements. Be sure to emphasize the scalloped edging by pinning out each leaf at the edges. Allow to dry thoroughly.

Sew up lengthways 15¾in (40cm) for sleeves on both sides. The leaves should work into each other to create a less noticeable seam.

If desired, weave a 35½in (90cm) piece of narrow ribbon approximately 1½in (4cm) up the sleeve edges to create the ability to cinch the sleeves in tighter. Weave in all ends. ⊕

Enchanted Shrug

"ELEGANT LACE LEAVES DANCE ALONG THIS ENCHANTING DESIGN"

Enchanted Shrug

Judy Furlong

Rose Shetland Shawl

Delicate cobweb shawl uses a delightful rose
motif to update a traditional design

Rose Shetland Shawl

THIS CONTEMPORARY SHAWL was inspired by the beautiful heritage shawls of Shetland, and designer Judy Furlong mixes traditional designs with a delicate rose motif.

"I especially love the delicate quality of these shawls, made possible by the very fine cobweb yarn and lacy openwork," says Judy.

"The traditional 'bead' stitch, used here in the central panels, is a particular favorite of mine and gives the whole garment a romantic, fragile feel."

The Rose shawl would be lovely worn over bare shoulders or a strappy summer or evening dress. Judy has used Jamieson & Smith 1ply Cobweb yarn, available in six shades, including black, which would give quite a different and dramatic look to the shawl. "This yarn is a great choice because it is very inexpensive and knot-free!" says Judy.

"Other than grafting, no special techniques are used here," Judy comments. "Typical of all Shetland shawls, casting on and off is kept to an absolute minimum, relying on picking up stitches and grafting to avoid seams."

STITCH PATTERNS

VANDYKE BORDER (traditional design)
Row 1: Sl 1P, K2, yo, K2tog, yo twice (yarn is wound right round the needle), K2tog.
Row 2: Yo (bring yarn fwd and hold RH needle behind the yarn and in front of first st as if to knit, then take yarn over the top of the RH needle ready for the knit st), K2, P1, K2, yo, K2tog, K1.
Row 3: Sl 1P, K2, yo, K2tog, K4.
Row 4: K6, yo, K2tog, K1.
Row 5: Sl 1P, K2, yo, K2tog, (yo twice, K2tog) twice.
Row 6: (K2, P1) twice, K2, yo, K2tog, K1.
Row 7: Sl 1P, K2, yo, K2tog, K6.
Row 8: K8, yo, K2tog, K1.
Row 9: Sl 1P, K2, yo, K2tog, (yo twice, K2tog) three times.
Row 10: (K2, P1) three times, K2, yo, K2tog, K1.
Row 11: Sl 1P, K2, yo, K2tog, K9.
Row 12: Cast off 7sts loosely. K until 4 sts on RH needle, yo, K2tog, K1.

FAGGOTTING & EYELET BORDER (RIGHT EDGE)
Row 1 (RS): Sl 1P, K2, (yo, K2tog) twice.
Row 2: K4, yo, K2tog, K1.

FAGGOTTING & EYELET BORDER (LEFT EDGE)
Row 1 (RS): (K2tog, yo) twice, K3.
Row 2: Sl 1P, K2, yo, K4.

BEAD STITCH (traditional design)
Row 1: K2, *yo, Sl1, K2tog, psso, yo, K3, repeat from * to last 5 sts, yo, Sl 1, K2tog, psso, yo, K2.
Row 2: K1, K2tog, *yo, K1, yo, K2tog, K1, ▶

SIZE

Length along straight edge: 64in (162½cm)
Nape of neck to lower edge: 20¾in (52½cm)

YARN

This project was stitched with **Jamieson & Smith** 1ply Cobweb (US: lace weight) (100% wool); ⅞oz/25g, 383yds/350m
4 balls in White

NEEDLES

1 pair 3mm (UK 11/US 2-3) knitting needles plus 1 spare 3mm needle

GAUGE

24 sts and 40 rows to 4in (10cm) worked over pattern using 3mm needles, after dressing.

NOTES

Read the chart for the Rose motif from right to left. Only RS rows are given as all WS rows of motif are purl.

The shawl is worked in stockinette stitch with a garter stitch lace border.

When picking up sts from the edge of the Vandyke border, pick up one loop only from every edge st along the edging. As the first st of every row was slipped, there will be 1 edge st to every 2 rows.

Put contrasting colored cloth over your lap to show up the work more clearly and work in good light.

If you drop a stitch, quickly lay the work over a contrasting colored surface without stretching it out (this might unravel the dropped sts) and catch the dropped sts with a finer needle or safety pins. If they have unravelled, work them back up to the row you are on by following the chart. Don't panic if you find it difficult to exactly repair the damage or recreate the lost stitches – during the dressing process, you can pin out the mistake to look as close to the pattern as possible. Slight errors will never be noticed once the piece is finished.

To join in the next ball of yarn – or if your yarn breaks – secure the new thread by knitting with the remaining old 'tail' and the new ball for 5 or so sts. Trim off the ends after the shawl is finished and blocked. This is not the usual recommendation as it often creates a bulky, visible set of stitches, but seems to be effective in this case because the yarn is so fine.

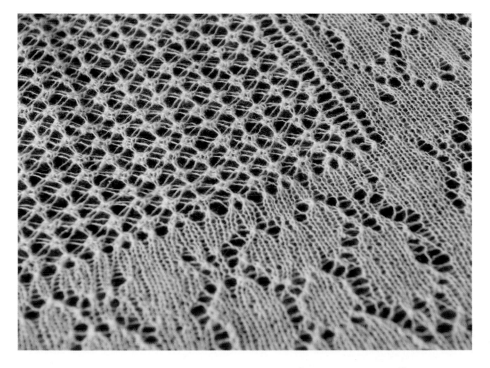

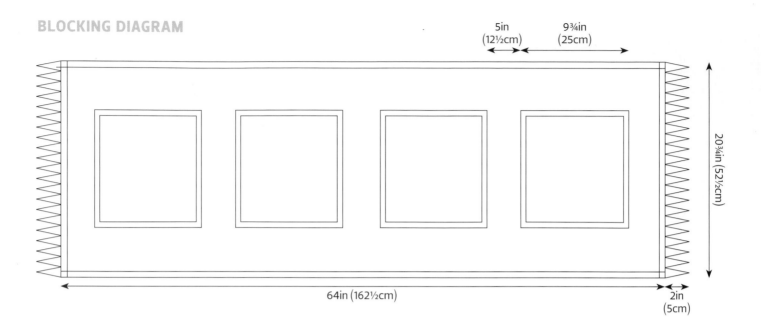

5in
(12½cm)

9¾in
(25cm)

20¾in (52½cm)

64in (162½cm)

2in
(5cm)

K2tog, repeat from * to last 4sts, yo, K1, yo, K2tog, K1.

Row 3: K2tog, yo, *K3, yo, Sl 1, K2tog, psso, yo, repeat from * to last 5 sts, K3, yo, K2tog.

Row 4: K1, yo, K2tog, K1, *K2tog, yo, K1, yo, K2tog, K1, repeat from * to last 3 sts, K2tog, yo, K1.

THE SHAWL

FIRST EDGING

Cast on 7 sts very loosely. It should be possible to stretch out the sts to 3cm.

Work all 12 rows of Vandyke Border 21 times (21 peaks).

Final row: Cast off 6 sts leaving remaining st on the RH needle.

MAIN SECTION

Row 1 (pick up): With last st from edging on the RH needle, pick up and knit 125 sts along long straight edge (126 sts on needle including st left after casting off).

Row 2: Sl 1P, K2tog, yo, K4, purl to last 7 sts, K4, yo, K2tog, K1.

SET PANELS

Row 3: Sl 1P, K2, (yo, K2tog) twice, place marker on needle, *K 28 (Row 3 of Rose motif), place marker on needle, repeat from * three more times, (K2tog, yo) twice, K3.

Row 4 (and all WS rows to Row 50): Sl 1P, K2tog, yo, K4, purl to last 7 sts, K4, yo, K2tog, K1, slipping markers.

Row 5: Sl 1P, K2, (yo, K2tog) twice, work row 5 of Rose motif 4 times, (K2tog, yo) twice, K3, slipping markers.

Row 6: As Row 4.

Row 7: Sl 1P, K2, (yo, K2tog) twice, work next row of Rose motif 4 times, (K2tog, yo) twice, K3, slipping markers.

Row 8: As Row 4.

Repeat Rows 7 and 8 until all 50 rows of the Rose motif have been completed finishing with:

Row 50: As Row 4, removing the middle marker.

Row 51 (eyelets): Sl 1P, K2, (yo, K2tog) twice, K 28 (Row 1 of Rose motif) (yo, K2tog) 28 times, K28 (Row 1 of Rose motif), (K2tog, yo) twice, K3.

Row 52: Sl 1P, K2tog, yo, K4, purl to last 7 sts, K4, yo, K2tog, K1.

Row 53 (start of Bead stitch panel): Sl 1P, K2, (yo, K2tog) twice, slip marker, K28 (Row 3 of Rose motif), slip marker, (yo, K2tog tbl) twice, K1, *yo, Sl 1, K2tog, psso, yo, K3, repeat from * 6 more times (9 sts before next marker), yo, Sl 1, K2tog, psso, yo, K2, (yo, K2tog tbl) twice, slip marker, K28 (Row 3 of Rose motif), (K2tog, yo) twice, K3.

Row 54: Sl 1P, K2tog, yo, K4, slip marker, P28, slip marker, P4, K1, K2tog, *yo, K1, yo, K2tog, K1, K2tog, repeat from * to last 7sts before marker, yo, K1, yo, K2tog, K1, P3, slip marker, P28, slip marker, K4, yo, K2tog, K1.

Row 55: Sl 1P, K2, (yo, K2tog) twice, work row 5 of Rose motif once, slip marker, yo, K2tog tbl, yo, Sl 1, K2tog, psso, yo, *K3, yo, Sl 1, K2tog, psso, yo, repeat from * to last 9 sts before marker, K3, yo, K2tog, (yo, K2tog tbl) twice, slip marker, work row 5 of Rose motif once, K2tog, yo, K2tog, yo, K3.

Row 56: Sl 1P, K2tog, yo, K4, P28, slip marker, P 4, K1, *yo, K2tog, K1, K2tog, yo, K1, repeat from * to last 3 sts before marker, P3, slip marker, P28, slip marker, K4, yo, K2tog, K1.

Row 57: Sl 1P, K2, (yo, K2tog) twice, work next row of Rose motif once, slip marker, (yo, K2tog tbl) twice, K1, *yo, Sl 1, K2tog, psso, yo, K3, repeat from * 6 more times (9 sts before next marker), yo, Sl 1, K2tog, psso, yo, K2, (yo, K2tog tbl) twice, slip marker, work next row of Rose motif once, (K2tog, yo) twice, K3.

Row 58: Sl 1P, K2tog, yo, K4, P 28, slip marker, P4, K1, K2tog, *yo, K1, yo, K2tog, K1, K2tog, repeat from * to last 7sts before next marker, yo, K1, yo, K2tog, K1, P3, slip marker, P28, slip marker, K4, yo, K2tog, K1.

Row 59: Sl 1P, K2, (yo, K2tog) twice, work next row of Rose motif once, slip marker, yo, K2tog tbl, yo, Sl 1, K2tog, psso, yo, *K3, yo, Sl 1, K2tog, psso, yo, repeat from * to last 9 sts before next marker, K3, yo, K2tog, (yo, K2tog tbl) twice, slip marker, work next row of Rose motif once, K2tog, yo, K2tog, yo, K3.

CHART

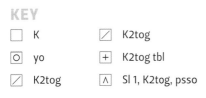

Only RS rows are shown as all WS rows are purl

KEY

□	K	╱	K2tog
O	yo	+	K2tog tbl
╱	K2tog	∧	Sl 1, K2tog, psso

Row 60: Sl 1P, K2tog, yo, K4, P 28, slip marker, P 4, K1, *yo, K2tog, K1, K2tog, yo, K1, repeat from * to last 3 sts before marker, P 3, slip marker, P28, slip marker, K4, yo, K2tog, K1.

Repeat Rows 57 to 60 inclusive for a further 21 times, then rows 57 to 59 inclusive once, ending after a row 47 of Rose motif .
Row 148: Sl 1P, K2tog, yo, K4, P 28, slip marker, P 56, slip marker, P 28, slip marker, K4, yo, K2tog, K1.
Row 149 (eyelet row): Sl 1P, K2, (yo, K2tog) twice, K 28 (Row 49 of Rose motif), (yo, K2tog) 28 times, K 28 (Row 49 of Rose motif), (K2tog, yo) twice, K3.
Row 150: Sl 1P, K2tog, yo, K4, P 28, slip marker, P 28, put marker on needle, (P 28, slip marker) twice, K4, yo, K2tog, K1.
Row 151: Sl 1P, K2, (yo, K2tog) twice, slip marker, *K 28 (Row 1 of Rose motif), slip marker, repeat from * three more times, (K2tog, yo) twice, K3.
Row 152: As Row 4.
Row 153: Sl 1P, K2, (yo, K2tog) twice, work next row of Rose motif 4 times, (K2tog, yo) twice, K3, slipping markers.
Row 154: As Row 4.
Repeat Rows 153 and 154 until all 50 rows of the Rose motif have been completed finishing with:
Row 200: As Row 4, removing the middle marker.
Repeat Rows 51 to 200 two more times.
Repeat Rows 51 to 150 one more time

(four bead st panels completed).
Repeat Rows 151 to 154.
Repeat Rows 153 and 154 until 48 rows of Rose motif have been completed.
Break off yarn and leave these sts on a needle to be grafted to the second edging.

SECOND EDGING
Work exactly as for First Edging, finishing at the end of Main section, Row 1 (pick up). There should be 126 sts on needle. Follow the instructions above to graft these sts to the 126 sts left after completing the Main section of the shawl.

FINISHING
Darn in any remaining loose ends.

DRESSING
To create the open lace pattern, the shawl must be 'dressed' as follows:
    Hand wash in warm water using a mild hand-wash detergent following the instructions on the ball band. This removes any loose dyes. Rinse thoroughly in several changes of water at the same temperature.
    Roll carefully in a towel, without wringing, to remove excess moisture.
    Pin out according to the dressing diagram. This is most easily achieved on a sheet laid on the floor. If space does not permit the shawl to be pinned out fully, pin out half then fold the other half over and re-pin to hold both edges.
    Allow the shawl to dry completely – this usually means leaving it overnight. ⊕

Vandyke border is worked as a strip before main section stitches are picked up along the length

In detail
Grafting the panels

Hold the two pieces with wrong sides facing each other. Thread tapestry needle with the yarn attached to the shawl and pass needle through first st, front needle as if to purl. Pass needle through first st, back needle as if to knit. *Pass needle through first st, front needle as if to knit and slip st off needle, pass needle through second st, front needle as if to purl. Pass needle through first st, back needle as if to purl and slip st off needle, pass needle through second st, back needle as if to knit. Rep from * until all sts have been slipped off needles, then weave in the end and trim.

66 THIS DELICATE YARN WILL CREATE A STUNNING SHAWL TO TREASURE 99

Quick lace

ELSA CASE

Judy Furlong

Fontaine Collar

A dainty accessory for all seasons, this collar
has an exquisite trailing leaf design

THIS PRETTY collar, designed by Judy Furlong, would add a touch of glamour to even the plainest top. The shape allows it to be worn in many ways – it can be held in place with a stunning brooch or with buttons sewn together as 'cufflinks'.

The collar combines a variation of a classic trailing leaf design with a fairly simple edging pattern. "Although the bulk of the garment is straightforward to knit, there are a few challenges, such as the nupps along the outer edge and working double yarnovers," says Judy.

MAIN SECTION

Using 4mm needles, cast on 9 sts. Work rows 1–36 from Chart once, then repeat the 28 row motif 10 times in total. Finally work the last 54 rows from Chart once. On the last row, cast off only two sts and transfer the remaining 9 sts to a stitch holder.

NECK EDGE

Wind off approx 5½yds (500cm) of yarn and using this tail, with RS facing, and 3.75mm circular needle, pick up and knit 9 sts from cast-on edge as marked on the Chart. Continuing along the inside edge (the edge without the nupps), pick up and knit 264 sts (approx 6 sts in every 7 row ends) finishing at the last row of Chart. Slip rem 9 sts from st holder onto the same circular

needle beside the picked-up sts.

SHAPING THE BEGINNING EDGE

Return to the beginning of the row and with RS facing and the main ball of yarn, continue as foll:

Short row pair 1: K1 tbl, w&t, P1.
Short row pair 2: K1 tbl, P1, K1 tbl, w&t, P1, K1 tbl, P1.
Short row pair 3: K1 tbl, (P1, K1 tbl) twice, w&t, (P1, K1 tbl) twice, P1.
Short row pair 4: K1 tbl, (P1, K1 tbl) three times, w&t, (P1, K1 tbl) three times, P1.
Short row pair 5: K1 tbl, (P1, K1 tbl) four times, w&t, (P1, K1 tbl) four times, P1.

MAIN SECTION

Row 1 (RS): K1 tbl, P1, K1 tbl, (yo, K2tog tbl) three times, P1, K2tog tbl, turn.
Row 2: Slip 1 st from RH to LH needle wyif, P2tog, K1 tbl, P1, (K1, P1) three times, K1 tbl, P1.
Repeat the last two rows until all the sts picked up along the inner edge have been incorporated into the Neck Edge ending with a Row 2 (20 sts remain including the final 9 sts of the collar main section).

SHAPING THE ENDING EDGE

Short row pair 1: K1 tbl, (P1, K1 tbl) four times, w&t, (P1, K1 tbl) four times, P1.
Short row pair 2: K1 tbl, (P1, K1 tbl) three times, w&t, (P1, K1 tbl) three times, P1.
Short row pair 3: K1 tbl, (P1, K1 tbl) twice, w&t, (P1, K1 tbl) twice, P1.
Short row pair 4: K1 tbl, P1, K1 tbl, w&t, ▶

SIZE

Maximum width: 6½in (16cm)
Length of inner curve: 39½in (100cm)
The buttons are not sewn on, so placement of the finished collar is fully adjustable.

YARN

This project was stitched with **Louisa Harding** Grace Hand Dyed, DK (US: sport weight) (50% merino wool, 50% silk); 1¾oz/50g, 109yds/100m
Shade 15: 3 x 50g hanks
Unfortunately, this color is now discontinued, but there are plenty of other colors available.

NEEDLES & ACCESSORIES

1 pair 4mm (UK 8/US 6) knitting needles.
1 pair 3.75mm (UK 9/US 5) knitting needles
1 set 3.75mm (UK 9/US 5) 80cm circular knitting needles
4 x 9mm buttons with shanks (optional)

GAUGE

22 sts and 30 rows to 4in (10cm) over st st using 4mm needles

SPECIAL ABBREVIATIONS

5-st nupp: K1, yo, K1, yo, K1 all into same stitch. It is important to work these loosely so that the P5tog on the next row is possible.
P5tog: Purl 5 stitches together, thus completing the nupp. If this is hard to do, try using a fine double-pointed needle to pull the loop through all 5 stitches and place the loop onto the working needle.

BLOCKING DIAGRAM

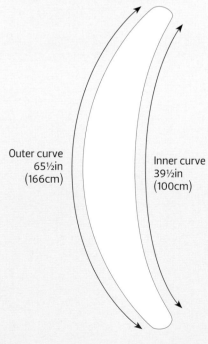

Outer curve 65½in (166cm)

Inner curve 39½in (100cm)

❝ CLEVER SHAPING ALLOWS THIS PRETTY COLLAR TO BE WORN MANY DIFFERENT WAYS ❞

Button fixtures can be moved along eyelet edge

P1, K1 tbl, P1.

Short row pair 5: K1 tbl, w&t, P1.

Row 6: (K1 tbl, P1) five times, K2tog tbl, P4, K1, yo, 5-st nupp, K2tog tbl.

Row 7: P1, P5tog, P1, K2tog, yarn back, Sl 1 purlwise, turn.

Short edging row 1(RS): Yfwd, P2tog, yo, 5-st nupp, K2tog tbl.

Short edging row 2 (WS): P1, P5tog, P1, K2tog, yfwd, Sl 1 purlwise, turn.

Repeat last two rows 5 more times.

Short edging row 13: yfwd, P2tog, yo, 5-st nupp, K2tog tbl.

Short edging row 14: P1, P5tog, P1, K2tog. 4 sts.

Short edging row 15: Sl 1 knitwise, yo, 5-st nupp, K2tog tbl.

Short edging row 16: P1, P5tog, pass first st over 2nd to cast off 1 st, P2tog, pass first st over 2nd to cast off 1 st, cut yarn, draw through remaining st and fasten off.

FINISHING

Darn in loose ends.

Block the collar gently as follows (avoid pressing as it will flatten the silk too much): Soak the collar for around 20 minutes in lukewarm water (following any ball band instructions), gently roll in a clean towel to remove excess water and spread out and shape according to blocking diagram. Smooth out the 'leaves', slightly overlapping their lower outside edges with the cast-off section of the previous leaf.

To enhance the three-dimensional effect, pinch up the stalk sections. Allow the collar to dry thoroughly.

MAKING 'CUFFLINKS'

Thread two buttons on the same yarn, make a slip knot in the end and pull up the buttons close together. Fasten off yarn securely. Use the yarn over holes in the collar edging as buttonholes. ⊕

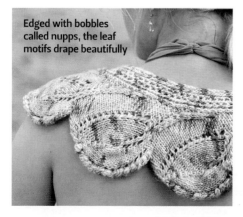

Edged with bobbles called nupps, the leaf motifs drape beautifully

Fontaine Collar

CHART

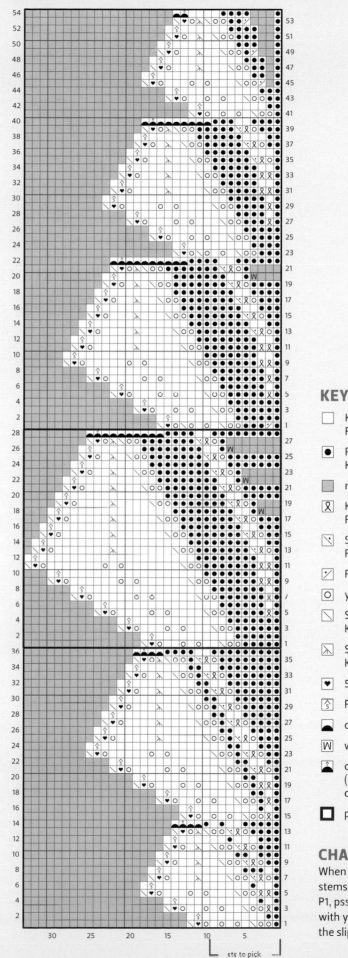

KEY

☐	K on RS, P on WS
●	P on RS, K on WS
▨	no stitch
⼋	K tbl on RS, P tbl on WS
⊼	Sl 1 purlwise, P1, psso
⟋	P2tog
O	yo
⟍	Sl 1 knitwise, K1, psso
⅄	Sl 1 knitwise, K2tog, psso
♥	5-st nupp
⤊	P5tog
▬	cast off knitwise
W	w&t
⛰	cast off nupp (P5tog and cast off)
☐	pattern repeat

CHART NOTE

When working the leaf stems, the Sl 1 purlwise, P1, psso should be worked with yarn held behind for the slipped stitch.

sts to pick up on edging

Ann Kingstone
Elsa Case

Carry your laptop or iPad in style
with this colorful lace case featuring an
intriguing double-layered construction

Elsa Case

Ann Kingstone
Elsa Case

SIZE
11 x 9in (28cm x 23cm) (33cm x 28cm:
39cm x 28cm:45cm x 37cm)

YARN
This project was stitched with the
following yarns.
Jamieson & Smith Shetland Aran, aran
weight (US: heavy worsted) (100% Shetland
wool); 1¾oz/50g, 98yds/90m
A Light green (BSS80) 2 (2:3:4) balls.
B Orange (BSS8) 1 ball all sizes.
Jamieson & Smith 2ply lace weight (US: lace
weight) (100% wool); ⅞oz/25g, 185yds/169m
C Royal blue (L17) 1 (1:1:2) balls (unfortunately,
this color has now been discontinued,
but there are plenty of other blues available
in the range.

NEEDLES & ACCESSORIES
1 set 3.5mm (UK 9-10/US 3) circular needles,
23½in (60cm) long
1 set 5mm (UK 6/US 8) circular needles,
23½in (60cm) long
1 set 4mm (UK 8/US 6) circular needles or
double-pointed needles (DPNs) for the applied
i-cord top and bottom edgings
2 small wooden closure toggles

GAUGE
22 sts and 32 rounds to 4in (10cm) over
blocked lace pattern using 3.25mm needles
16.5 sts and 21 rounds to 4in (10cm) over
blocked st st using 5mm needles

I-CORD INSTRUCTIONS
Create an i-cord by working the same small
number of stitches over and over again, each
time slipping the stitches worked from the
right-hand needle to the left-hand needle.
When you have slipped your stitches back to
the left-hand needle, pull the working yarn
tight, to avoid creating a ladder.
This i-cord is worked as foll:

GADGET FANS know that expensive
pieces such as laptops and iPads need
protecting, but shop-bought covers can
be a little dull. This wonderful design by
Ann Kingstone is both practical and
beautiful, combining a stockinette
stitch inner bag with a lacy outer layer
in a contrasting color.

It's written in four sizes, and uses
some interesting techniques including
Turkish cast-on for a seamless effect,
and an applied i-cord edging. Ann
has used two wools from Jamieson
& Smith, the Shetland Aran and the
2ply Lace Weight, and a toggle closure.

NOTES
The side edgings are worked separately, so
you will require two separate balls of yarn
B. Prepare for this by winding a small ball
off the main ball before starting and hold it
in reserve until it is required.

The side edgings are intarsia i-cord: each
time you reach them, bring yarn B back
behind the stitches from where it was left
during the previous round, then knit the
stitches as normal, pulling the yarn tight
when working the first stitch.

INNER BAG
Using 5mm needles and yarn A cast on
92 (110:130:148) sts using either the Turkish

cast-on method or Judy's Magic Cast-On.
You can learn more about these two
cast-on methods in detail *http://theknitter.
themakingspot.com/category/tags/
cast-ons.*

Join to knit in the round, being careful not
to twist work, and place marker to indicate
start of round.
Knit every round, to create a st st fabric,
working until the bag measures 21
(26:26:35)cm from the cast-on edge.

Next round: K2tog twice, knit
38 (47:57:66), SSK twice, K2tog twice,
K38 (47:57:66), SSK twice.
84 (102:122:140) sts.

TOP EDGING
With 4mm needles and yarn B cast on 4 sts
and work an applied i-cord around the
remaining 84 (102:122:140) sts of the top
edging as follows:
*K3, yo, Sl 1, K1, pass the yo and the slipped
sts over the last knitted st, slip 4 sts back to
the working needle; rep from * until all the
sts have been worked.
Break off the yarn leaving a short tail.
Thread this onto a darning needle and graft
the last 4 sts to the first 4 sts of the edging.

LACE OVERBAG
Turn the bag so the opening is now at the
bottom, facing you. You will now work the

lace overbag back over the inner bag with
the right side of the inner bag facing you.

All sts for the next section are picked up and
and knitted through both the i-cord st
(yarn B) and its base st (yarn A).
Starting at the grafted sts, and using
3.5mm needles, pick up and knit sts
through the edging as follows, holding the
yarns to the inside of the bag:
*Using yarn B, pick up and knit 3 sts.
Change to yarn C, pick up and knit 3 (2:4:3)
sts, (M1, pick up and knit 2) 18 (23:27:32)
times; repeat from * once more.
120 (148:176:204) sts

Knit one round plain.

Now, following the instructions for the
number of repeats given for your size
below, work from the lace chart as foll:
*K3 in yarn B, then work the lace pattern as
charted in yarn C, working the side sts,
working the main lace repeat 3 (4:5:6)
times and then working the second set of
side sts. You should now have reached the
next 3 yarn B sts; repeat from * once more.

Use the reserved supply of yarn B for the
second set of yarn B sts. In all rounds
carry yarn C behind the yarn B sts to work
the lace on both sides of the bag with the
same yarn ball.

CHART

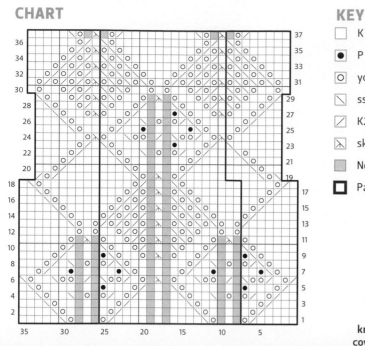

KEY

- ☐ K
- ● P
- ⊙ yo
- ╲ ssk
- ╱ K2tog
- ⋌ sk2P
- ▨ No stitch
- ◻ Pattern repeat

Outer lacy layer and i-cord edging are knitted onto the inner cover at the same time

CHART INSTRUCTIONS

Starting from round 1 of the lace chart work 1 repeat of rounds 1 to 37.

Then, starting from round 2 for all subsequent rounds, work 1 (2:2:2) more repeats of the lace chart, ending with round 29 (11:11:37).
65(83:83:109) rounds in lace pattern with i-cord side edgings worked.

After completing the required number of lace pattern rounds, knit one round plain, continuing the i-cord side edgings as established, then work a decrease round as foll:
*K3 in yarn B, then in yarn C knit 3 (2:4:3) sts, (K2tog, K1) 18 (23:27:32) times; repeat from * to end. 84(102:122:140) sts.

BOTTOM EDGING

Now transfer both needles to your left hand so that you are holding them ready to work a three-needle cast-off.

With the 4mm needle and working solely with the yarn from the first set of side i-cord sts (yarn B), work applied i-cord while casting off the sts as follows:
*K2, Sl 1, yo, knit together the next front needle st with the next rear needle st, pass slipped st and yo over the st just worked, slip 3 sts back to the front left-hand needle; repeat from * until all the yarn C sts have been worked.
Break off the yarn leaving a short tail. Thread this onto a darning needle and use it to graft the i-cord sts from the edge now reached to the i-cord cast off sts just worked.

FINISHING

Weave in all ends. Block to required dimensions.

Take a toggle, and sew it onto one side of the rim opening at approx one-third of the way in from the side piping.
Using the 3.5mm needle and yarn B, make a length of two-stitch i-cord approx 1¼in (3cm) long, or the length required to snugly fasten around a toggle.
Sew the ends of the i-cord together to make a loop, then sew the loop to the rim opening opposite the toggle just placed.
In the same way, fasten another toggle and make a second i-cord loop, fastening one third of the way in from the other side piping. ⊕

Amanda Crawford
Abruzzi Capelet

Bring elegance to your outdoor wardrobe with this
pretty lacework capelet in a cashmere blend

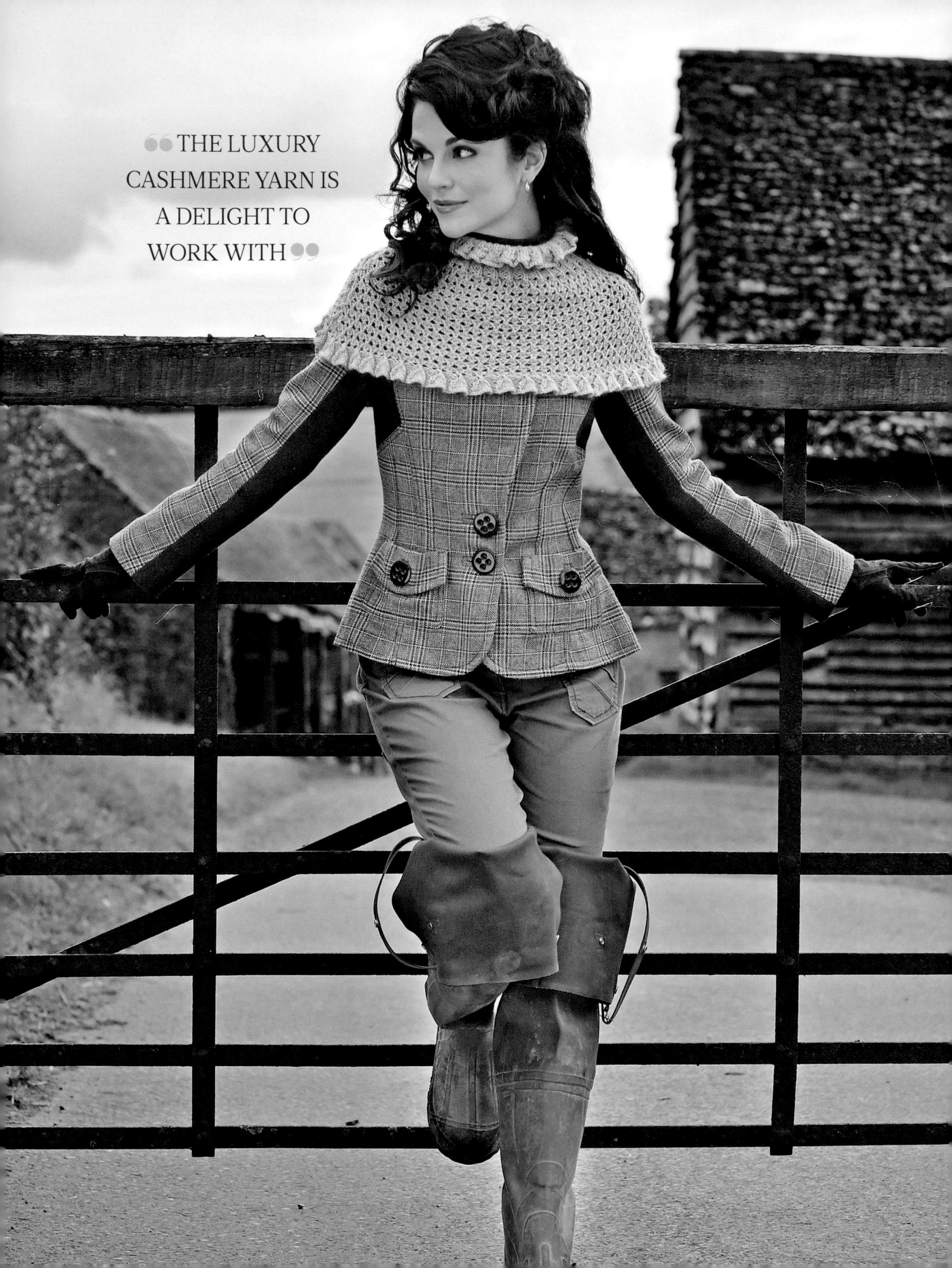
“THE LUXURY
CASHMERE YARN IS
A DELIGHT TO
WORK WITH”

Amanda Crawford
Abruzzi Capelet

SIZE

	XS	S	M	L	XL	
TO FIT BUST	81-86	86-90	90-96	102-108	112-116	cm
	32-34	34-36	36-38	40-42	44-46	in
ACTUAL CIRCUM-FERENCE	80	88	96	104	112	cm
	31½	34½	38	41	44	in

YARN

This project was stitched with **Schoppel Wolle** Cashmere Queen, worsted (45% merino wool, 35% cashmere, 20% silk); 1¾oz/50g, 153yds/140m

BEIGE MELLIERT	3	3	3	3	4	x50g BALLS

NEEDLES & ACCESSORIES

1 set 4mm (UK 8/US 6) circular knitting needles
Stitch markers

GAUGE

20 sts and 26 rows to 4in (10cm) over lace pattern using 4mm needles

NOTES

When working shaping decreases in a lace pattern, it is important to keep lace increases and decreases balanced. For example, if you don't have enough sts to work one of the yarn overs, work K2tog instead of K3tog. If in doubt, replace the partial lace repeat with st st.

IF YOU ADORE tailored fashion, the last thing you want to do when adding extra layers is to end up with an overly chunky, baggy look. You need something sleeker and more fitted, where the warmth is added through top-quality yarn – in fact, what you need is this cashmere capelet. It simply pulls straight over the head and sits perfectly around the shoulders and neck, with no fastening required. The luxury yarn is a delight to work with and creates a stunning finish.

Worked in the round and from the bottom-up, Amanda Crawford's elegant capelet pattern starts with a daffodil stitch edging, which complements the main lace pattern. This body lace pattern is worked over four stitches and eight rows, making it quite straightforward to memorize, so it should be a quick and simple knit. Decreases are then worked to give shaping to the neck, ending with a pretty ruffled edging.

Cashmere Queen from Schoppel Wolle is a soft, smooth yarn with an interesting construction. Without appearing to have a twist, the single ply yarn knits to a fabric with good stitch definition and a light halo. Cashmere is an ideal fiber for fine layers such as this, offering plenty of insulation and warmth without bulk, and the touch of merino and silk add even more luxury! It's the perfect choice for medium-weight lace projects like this one.

CAPELET

Using 4mm circular needle cast on 400 (440:480:520:560) sts. Join to work in the round, taking care not to twist sts. Place marker for beg of round.

Rounds 1 & 2: *P3, K7; rep from * to end.
Round 3: *P3, K2tog tbl, K3, K2tog; rep from * to end. 320 (352:384:416:448) sts.
Round 4: *P3, K5; rep from * to end.
Round 5: *P3, K2tog tbl, K1, K2tog; rep from * to end. 240 (264:288:312:336) sts.
Round 6: *P3, K3; rep from * to end.
Round 7: *P3, K3tog; rep from * to end. 160 (176:192:208:224) sts.
Round 8: *P3, K1; rep from * to end.
Round 9: *K3tog, yo, P1, yo; rep from * to end.
Rounds 10, 11 & 12: *P1, K3; rep from * to end.
Round 13: P1, yo, K3tog, yo; rep from * to end.
Rounds 14, 15 & 16: K2, P1, K1; rep from * to end.

Add a second marker to divide your stitches into two equal portions.
Last 8 rounds form lace patt. Cont in lace patt decreasing 1 st on each side of both markers on every 4th row until 112 (112:128:128:136) sts remain.
Work 4 rounds straight.
Next round: *K2tog, P2; rep from * to end. 84 (84:96:96:102) sts.

Next round: *K1, P2; rep from * to end.
Rep last round 13 more times.

Next round: *P1, K2; rep from * to end.

Rep last round 6 more times.

Next round: *(K1,P1, K1) into next st, K2; rep from * to end.
140 (140:160:160:170) sts.
Next round: *P3, K2; rep from * to end.
Next round: *P1, M1, P1, M1, P1, K2; rep from * to end. 196 (196:224:224:238) sts.
Next round: *P5, K2; rep from * to end.
Next round: *P1, M1, P3, M1, P1, K2; rep from * to end. 252 (252:288:288:306) sts.
Next round: *P7, K2; rep from * to end.

Cast off all sts. Weave in all ends. ⊕

The ruffled neck edging is created with a series of steep increases – simple but perfect.

Teva Durham

Marianne Purse

Lacy leaf patterning and a scalloped edging ensure this lacy bag stands out from the crowd

Marianne Purse

SIZE
One size. Approx 14in x 16½in at widest points (35cm x 42cm)

YARN
This project was stitched with
Loop-d-Loop by Teva Durham Birch, aran weight (US: heavy worsted) (65% cotton, 35% silk); 1¾oz/50g, 98yds/90m
Fuchsia (12) 3 x 50g balls

NEEDLES
1 pair 5mm (UK 6/US 8) needles
1 set 5mm (UK 6/US 8) circular needles, 15¾in (40cm) long

GAUGE
16 sts and 20 rows to 4in (10cm) over st st

ACCESSORIES
2 horseshoe bag handles, 4½ x 5½in (11½ x 14cm)
19½in (50cm) lining fabric and thread to match
Tailor's chalk

PATTERN NOTES
Front and Back worked separately for top, joined on chart row 15, then worked in round.

ALTERATIVE YARN
Rico Design Creative Cotton, aran weight (US: heavy worsted) (100% cotton); 1¾oz/50g, 93yds/85m. Use 3 x 50g balls in color Rose 00.
Debbie Bliss Eco Aran, aran weight (US: heavy worsted) (100% organic cotton); 1¾oz/50g, 82yds/75m. Use 4 x 50g balls in color Raspberry 25.

TEVA DURHAM loves to play with shape, and this lace bag uses a leaf motif to create its pretty outline. "The design is adapted from a small segment of the '*Rose of England*' Doily by Marianne Kinzel in her *Second Book of Modern Lace Knitting*," says Teva. "Doilies provide perfect wedge shapes for a handbag as they have a rate of increase built into the lace pattern. This bag features two pairs of leaves each on front and back, with a madeira-lace diamond pattern between the leaves. The angle of the leaves has a scalloping effect and I utilized the scallop edge of the pattern to form the bottom of the bag."

BAG TOP BACK
Cast on 40 sts.
Foundation row: Purl.
Row 1 (RS): Begin chart row 1, as foll: K1, *yo, K19; rep from * once, yo, K1. 43 sts.
Next and all WS rows: Purl.
Row 3: K1, *yo, K1, yo, K8, Sl1, K2tog, psso, K8; rep from * once, (yo, K1) twice. 45 sts.
Row 5: K1, *Sl1, K2tog, psso, yo, K7, Sl1, K2tog, psso, K7, yo; rep from * once, Sl1, K2tog, psso, K1. 39 sts.
Row 7: K1, *K1 tbl, yo, K1, yo, K6, Sl1, K2tog, psso, K6, yo, K1, yo; rep from * once, K1 tbl, K1. 43 sts.
Continue to work beg st, work chart rep twice, then work end sts as established.
Continue until chart row 13 is complete.

Purl WS row. Cut yarn and put on spare needle.

BAG TOP FRONT
Work as for Bag Top Back until chart row 13 is complete. 47 sts.
Purl WS row.

JOIN BAG FRONT AND BACK
Next row/Round 15: K1, *(K1 tbl, yo) 4 times, SSK, K2, yo, K2, Sl1, K2tog, psso, K2, yo, K2, K2tog, (yo, K1 tbl) 3 times*; rep from * to * once [2 sts remain], Sl1, take up Bag Top Back with RS facing and K2tog (working the last st of the Front together with the first st of the Back), psso, rep from * to * twice, Sl1, 1 st rem, then knit the last st tog with the first st of the Bag Front to join into round, psso, place marker before the resulting st of this dec for beg of round. 110 sts. (27 sts rep x 4, plus 1 st each edge where joined).
Knit 1 round.
Round 17: *Yo, Sl 1 [make sure this first st is the rem st from the join below], K2tog, psso, yo, K2, yo, K1 tbl, yo, K1, SSK, yo, Sl1, K2tog, psso, (yo, K1) twice, Sl1, K2tog, psso, (K1, yo) twice, Sl1, K2tog, psso, yo, K2tog, K1, yo, K1 tbl, yo, K2; rep from * 3 more times.
Next and all alternate rounds: Knit.
Continue to work chart as established 4 times across round. Note shaping is done within chart and stitch number varies.
Cont to work from chart until Round 61 is complete. 160 sts.
Knit 6 rounds.
Cast off.

Lacy leaves are a classic motif — and it's easy to see why

CHART

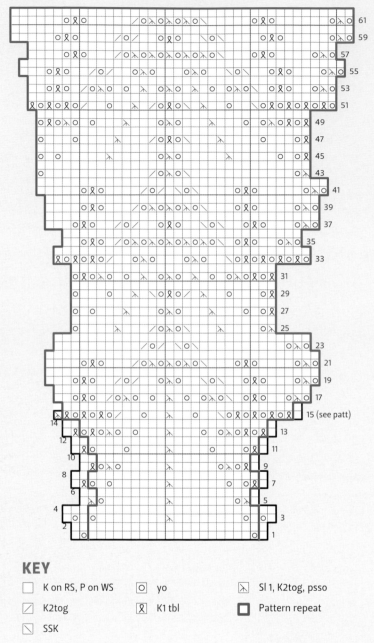

KEY

☐	K on RS, P on WS	○	yo	⋏	Sl 1, K2tog, psso
╱	K2tog	Ձ	K1 tbl	☐	Pattern repeat
╲	SSK				

Working the leaf motif to the edge of the knitting creates a scalloped effect

FINISHING

Block lightly.

Sew Front cast-off edge to Back cast-off edge to form bag bottom (stitch pattern will scallop).

Center handles at top of bag. With yarn and tapestry needle, sew one to Front and one to Back (handle ends should align with the decreases of chart). Attaching handles before lining will help to determine the drape of top of bag and the shape of lining.

LINING

Cut rectangle of lining fabric as wide as widest part of bag plus ½in (1¼cm) each side for seam allowance, and twice the height of bag plus 2in (5cm). Fold top edge to bottom edge - the center will be the base of the bag. Pinch in bottom corners to match shape of bag, gathering extra fabric at side into seam. Pin and sew each side, leaving 10cm open at top plus ½in (1¼cm) seam allowance. Place lining inside bag and use tailor's chalk to outline the shape of the Top Front and Top Back, adding seam allowance.

Cut excess fabric and press seam allowance to WS. Whip-stitch the lining to each top edge and open side edge. ⊕

“ THE LACY LEAF OUTLINES WORK PERFECTLY TO CREATE THE SHAPE OF THE BAG ”

Kirstie McLeod

Elwood Hat

Rustle up this quick-knit hat with lace and cable
patterning, using fingering yarn from your stash

WE'VE ALL GOT those odd balls of yarn in our stash that were "just calling to you". Yarns you just had to buy, but with no firm design in mind. Does this sound familiar? Well, if you're looking for a great pattern to put your yarn to good use, then this hat design, using a chevron lace stitch interspersed with cabling, is the perfect choice. It uses the tubular cast-on method, which is lovely and stretchy for a comfy fit.

Kirstie McLeod, the designer, tells us: "I really wanted to come up with a cozy hat pattern, something that's interesting to knit but also that would be fairly speedy! I had some Jamieson and Smith Jumper Weight yarn left over from another project, so I figured this would be the perfect way to use it up."

We've given you some ideas for other 4ply yarns you could use (right) and it would make a great gift knit, especially as it's the sort of shape that suits so many people. So get hunting through your stash and cast on the perfect lace stashbuster.

LACE AND CABLE PATTERN

Over 21 sts and 8 rows.
Rnd 1: P3, K6, P3, yo, Sl1, K1, psso, K5, K2tog, yo.
Rnd 2 and all even rounds: P3, K6, P3, K9.
Rnd 3: P3, K6, P3, K1, yo, Sl1, K1, psso, K3, K2tog, yo, K1.
Rnd 5: P3, K6, P3, K2, yo, Sl1, K1, psso, K1, K2tog, yo, K2.
Rnd 7: P3, C6F, P3, K3, yo, Sl1, K2tog, psso, yo, K3.
Rnd 8: P3, K6, P3, K9.

HAT

Using some waste yarn and 3.75mm circular needle or DPNs work a tubular cast on as folls:
Cast on 73 sts. Join to work in the round and work 5 rounds in st st. Change to the main yarn and work 4 more rounds in st st.
Next rnd: *K1, bring yarn to front, pick up the loop of main yarn, from the first row, between the 2 waste yarn sts and purl it, yb; rep from * to the end of the round. 146 sts.

Next rnd: *K1, P1; rep from * to end. Continue working a 1x1 rib as set above for 9 further rounds, inc 1 st at end of last round. 147 sts.
Remove waste yarn from cast-on edge.

Start to work lace and cable pattern (from chart or written instructions), repeating motif 7 times each round.

Continue until 96 rounds have been worked in pattern (12 repeats).

Rnd 1: *P2tog, P1, K6, P3, yo, Sl1, K1, psso, K5, K2tog, yo; rep from * to end of round. 140 sts.
Rnd 2: *P2, K6, P3, K9; rep from * to end.
Rnd 3: *P2, K6, P2tog, P1, K1, yo, Sl1, K1, psso, K3, K2tog, yo, K1; rep from * to end of round. 133 sts.
Rnd 4: *P2, K6, P2, K9; rep from * to end of round.
Rnd 5: *P2tog, K6, P2, K2, yo, Sl1, K1, psso, K1, K2tog, yo, K2; rep from * to end of round. 126 sts.
Rnd 6: *P1, K6, P2, K9; rep from * to end of round.
Rnd 7: *P1, C6F, P2tog, K3, yo, Sl1, K2tog, psso, yo, K3; rep from * to end of round. 119 sts.
Rnd 8: *P1, K1, Sl1, K1, psso, K3, P1, K9; rep from * to end of round. 112 sts.
Rnd 9: *P1, K2, K2tog, K1, P1, yo, Sl1, K1, psso, K5, K2tog, yo; rep from * to end. 105 sts.
Rnd 10: *P1, K4, P1, Sl1, K1, psso, K5, K2tog; rep from * to end. 91 sts.
Rnd 11: *P1, K4, P1, Sl1, K1, psso, K3, K2tog; rep from * to end. 77 sts.
Rnd 12: *P1, K4, P1, Sl1, K1, psso, K1, K2tog; rep from * to end. 63 sts.
Rnd 13: *P1, Sl1, K1, psso, K2tog, P1, K3; rep from * to end. 49 sts.
Rnd 14: *P1, K2, P1, Sl1, K2tog, psso; rep from * to end. 35 sts.

Thread yarn through sts and secure. Weave in all loose ends. Hand wash and re-shape while wet. ⊕

The tubular cast-on gives a nice stretchy edge to the ribbing

SIZE
One size - head circumference up to 21¼in (54cm)

YARN
This project was stitched with **Jamieson and Smith** 2ply Jumper Weight, knits as 4ply (US: fingering) (100% Shetland wool); ⅞oz/25g, 129yds/118m
Shade FC15; 3 x 25g balls

NEEDLES & ACCESSORIES
1 set 3.75mm (UK 9/ US 5) circular needles, 15¾in (40cm) long
1 set of four 3.75mm (UK 9/ US 5) double-pointed needles (optional)
Cable needle (cn)
Small quantity waste yarn

GAUGE
28 sts and 40 rows to 4in (10cm) over cable and lace pattern using 3.75mm needles

SPECIAL ABBREVIATIONS
C6F: Sl 3 sts to cn and hold at front, K3 and then K3 from cn

YARN SUBSTITUTION
When substituting a yarn, remember that you need to use something that will knit to the same gauge, and you will need the same total length of yarn for the pattern. For this hat, you will need approx 328yds (300m) of 4ply yarn.

Other yarns that you may like to try include:
Fyberspates Sheila's Sock (100% superwash merino; 365m/100g skeins) 1 skein needed
Debbie Bliss Rialto 4ply (100% extrafine merino; 180m/50g balls) 2 balls needed
Artesano Alpaca 4ply (100% pure superfine alpaca; 184m/50g balls) 2 balls needed
Stylecraft Life 4ply (75% acrylic, 25% wool; 450m/100g balls) 1 ball needed

CHART

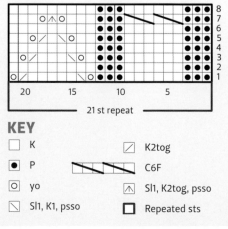

21 st repeat

KEY
☐ K
● P
○ yo
╲ Sl1, K1, psso
╱ K2tog
〈〉 C6F
⩔ Sl1, K2tog, psso
☐ Repeated sts

Ann Kingstone
Pearl Mittens

Delicate lacy wristwarmers are knitted in
a variegated cashmere-merino blend

SIZE

SIZE	S	M	L	
TO FIT HAND CIRCUMFERENCE	16½	19	21½	cm
	6½	7½	8½	in

YARN

This project was stitched with **Skein Queen** Blush, Heavy 4ply weight (US: fingering) (80% merino, 20% cashmere); 3½oz/100g, 430yds/393m. Color is Rosehip; 1 x 100g skein (all sizes). This was a one-off color that is now sold out;

NEEDLES & ACCESSORIES

1 set 2.5mm (UK 13-12/US 1-2) needles for your preferred method of small-diameter circular knitting; either DPNs, two medium circular needles, or one long circular (for Magic Loop method)
2 x 20mm buttons (the buttons we used are from The Button Company)
Waste 4ply yarn for the provisional cast-on and for setting up the afterthought thumb.

GAUGE

34 sts and 40 rows/rounds to 4in (10cm) over stockinette stitch

SPECIAL ABBREVIATIONS

MB: Make bobble. ([K1, yo] twice, K1) all into the same stitch, turn, P5, turn, K5, turn, P5, turn, K5, pass preceding four stitches over the last stitch worked.

THESE WRISTWARMERS are perfect for keeping your hands warm when there's a chill in the air, and thanks to Ann Kingstone's delicate design, you won't sacrifice elegance for warmth.

The combination of a pretty diamond lace pattern with an edging of bobbles and mesh lace, mean that these will make an interesting knit that will be finished quickly. They're also great value because you'll get two pairs from one skein of Blush yarn.

MITTENS

Using a provisional method, cast on 44 (50:56) sts then work back and forth in flat knitting as foll:
Set-up row: P11 (14:17), P2tog, yo, P16, P2tog, yo, purl to end.
Row 1 (RS): K11 (14:17), SSK, yo, K3, MB, K3, yo, SSK, K2tog, yo, K3, MB, K1, SSK, yo, knit to end.
Row 2: As set-up row.
Row 3: K11 (14:17), SSK, yo, K5, K2tog, yo, K4, yo, SSK, K3, SSK, yo, knit to end.
Row 4: As set-up row.
Row 5: K11 (14:17), SSK, yo, K4, K2tog, yo, K1, K2tog, yo twice, SSK, K1, yo, SSK, K2, SSK, yo, knit to end.
Row 6: P11 (14:17), P2tog, yo, P9, K1, P6, P2tog, yo, purl to end.
Row 7: K11 (14:17), SSK, yo, K3, K2tog, yo, K8, yo, SSK, K1, SSK, yo, knit to end.
Row 8: As set-up row.
Row 9: K11 (14:17), SSK, yo, K2, K2tog, yo, K1, K2tog, yo twice, SSK, K2tog, yo twice, SSK, K1, yo, SSK, SSK, yo, knit to end.
Row 10: P11 (14:17), P2tog, yo, P7, K1, P3, K1, P4, P2tog, yo, purl to end.

Row 11: K11 (14:17), SSK, yo, K4, yo, SSK, K6, K2tog, yo, K2, SSK, yo, knit to end.
Row 12: As set-up row.
Row 13: K11 (14:17), SSK, yo, K5, yo, SSK, K2tog, yo twice, SSK, K2tog, yo, K3, SSK, yo, knit to end.
Row 14: P11 (14:17), P2tog, yo, P9, K1, P6, P2tog, yo, purl to end.
Row 15: K11 (14:17), SSK, yo, K6, yo, SSK, K2, K2tog, yo, K4, SSK, yo, knit to end.
Row 16: As set-up row.
Row 17: As row 1.
Row 18: As set-up row.
Row 19: K0 (1:2), (K2tog) 5 (6:7) times, K1, SSK, yo, K5, K2tog, yo, K4, yo, SSK, K3, SSK, yo, K3, (K2tog) 5 (6:7) times, K0 (1:2). 34 (38:42) sts.
Row 20: P6 (8:10), P2tog, yo, P16, P2tog, yo, purl to end.
Row 21: K6 (8:10), SSK, yo, K4, K2tog, yo, K1, K2tog, yo twice, SSK, K1, yo, SSK, K2, SSK, yo, knit to end.
Row 22: P6 (8:10), P2tog, yo, P9, K1, P6, P2tog, yo, purl to end.
Row 23: K6 (8:10), SSK, yo, K3, K2tog, yo, K8, yo, SSK, K1, SSK, yo, knit to end.
Row 24: As row 20.
Row 25: K6 (8:10), SSK, yo, K2, K2tog, yo, K1, K2tog, yo twice, SSK, K2tog, yo twice, SSK, K1, yo, SSK, SSK, yo, knit to end.
Row 26: P6 (8:10), P2tog, yo, P7, K1, P3, K1, P4, P2tog, yo, purl to end.
Row 27: K6 (8:10), SSK, yo, K4, yo, SSK, K6, K2tog, yo, K2, SSK, yo, knit to end.
Row 28: As row 20.
Row 29: K6 (8:10), SSK, yo, K5, yo, SSK, K2tog, yo twice, SSK, K2tog, yo, K3, SSK, yo, knit to end.
Row 30: P6 (8:10), P2tog, yo, P9, K1, P6, P2tog, yo, purl to end.

Row 31: K6 (8:10), SSK, yo, K6, yo, SSK, K2, K2tog, yo, K4, SSK, yo, knit to end.
Row 32: As row 20.
Row 33: K6 (8:10), SSK, yo, K3, MB, K3, yo, SSK, K2tog, yo, K3, MB, K1, SSK, yo, knit to end.
Row 34: As row 20.
Row 35: K1 (2:3), (M1, K1) 5 (6:7) times, SSK, yo, K5, K2tog, yo, K4, yo, SSK, K3, SSK, yo, K3, (M1, K1) 5 (6:7) times, K0 (1:2). 44 (50:56) sts.

Join for knitting in the round, and K11 (14:17) to bring you to the beginning of the pattern panel (the pattern panel is also shown in the chart). The remainder of the mitten (excluding edgings) is knitted in the round and all rounds will begin at this point (at the beginning of the pattern panel). In all rounds, the pattern panel is knitted first and the remainder of the round is knitted plain, except in Round 32 when stitches are inserted to set up for the afterthought thumb.
Round 1: K2, yo, K2tog, K16, yo, K2tog, knit to end.
Round 2: SSK, yo, K4, K2tog, yo, K1, K2tog, yo twice, SSK, K1, yo, SSK, K2, SSK, yo, knit to end.
Round 3: K2, yo, K2tog, K6, P1, K9, yo, K2tog, knit to end.
Round 4: SSK, yo, K3, K2tog, yo, K8, SSK, K1, SSK, yo, knit to end.
Round 5: As round 1.
Round 6: SSK, yo, K2, K2tog, yo, K1, K2tog, yo twice, SSK, K2tog, yo twice, SSK, K1, yo, SSK twice, yo, knit to end.
Round 7: K2, yo, K2tog, K4, P1, K3, P1, K7, yo, K2tog, knit to end.
Round 8: SSK, yo, K4, yo, SSK, K6,

CHART

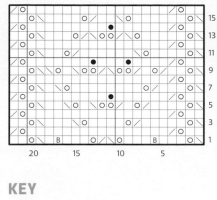

KEY

- ☐ K on RS, P on WS
- ⬛ P on RS, K on WS
- ╱ K2tog on RS, P2tog on WS
- ╲ SSK on RS, SSP on WS
- ○ yo
- B MB

K2tog, yo, K2, SSK, yo, knit to end.

Round 9: As round 1.

Round 10: SSK, yo, K5, yo, SSK, K2tog, yo twice, SSK, K2tog, yo, K3, SSK, yo, knit to end.

Round 11: K2, yo, K2tog, K6, P1, K9, yo, K2tog, knit to end.

Round 12: SSK, yo, K6, yo, SSK, K2, K2tog, yo, K4, SSK, yo, knit to end.

Round 13: As round 1.

Round 14: SSK, yo, K3, MB, K3, yo, SSK, K2tog, yo, K3, MB, K1, SSK, yo, knit to end.

Round 15: As round 1.

Round 16: SSK, yo, K5, K2tog, yo, K4, yo, SSK, K3, SSK, yo, knit to end.

Rounds 17 – 31: As rounds 1 – 15.

Round 32 (1st glove): SSK, yo, K5, K2tog, yo, K4, yo, SSK, K3, SSK, yo, K0 (2:4), drop main yarn, K10 with waste yarn, slip 10 sts back to passive (left-hand) needle, with main yarn knit to end.

Round 32 (2nd glove): SSK, yo, K5, K2tog, yo, K4, yo, SSK, K3, SSK, yo, knit to last 10 (12:14) sts, drop main yarn, K10 with waste yarn, slip 10 sts back to passive (left-hand) needle, with main yarn knit to end.

Rounds 33 – 48: As rounds 1 – 16.

Rounds 49 – 63: As rounds 1 – 15.

This completes the main mitten.
Without breaking off the yarn continue immediately with the top edging as foll: K2, *slip two sts back to passive needle, K1, Sl1, K1, psso; repeat from * until all stitches have been worked into the edging. Break

Pattern is given for three sizes, and in both written and charted formats

off yarn leaving a short tail for sewing in. Thread this onto a darning needle and use it to neatly join the end of the edging to the beginning, then weave it in to finish.

THUMB

Remove the waste yarn and pick up and knit the live sts from above and below the thumbhole. To minimize the risk of holes at the edges of the thumbhole, also pick up and knit 1 – 2 sts from loose strands here, knitting the strands tbl.
Knit 8 rounds then finish the thumb following the instructions for the top edging of the mitten.

BOTTOM EDGING

Place the provisional sts from the bottom of the mitten onto a spare needle and hold them ready to be worked when you reach them in the instructions that follow.
Cast on 2 sts, then commencing at the top of the wrist opening apply the edging as follows:

First side of opening: *Slip two sts to passive needle, K1, Sl1, pick up and knit one st from the edge of the opening, psso;

repeat from * until you reach the provisional sts.

Bottom edge: *Slip two sts back to passive needle, K1, Sl1, K1, psso; repeat from * until all the provisional sts have been worked.

Second side of the opening: *Slip two sts back to passive needle, K1, Sl1, pick up and knit one st from the edge of the opening, psso; repeat from * until 1/2in (1 1/2cm) beyond the edge of the decrease row in the main mitten.

At this point work the buttonhole as follows: *Sl two sts back to the passive needle, K2, repeat from * until you have worked 1/4in (1cm) of two-stitch i-cord, then continue with the applied edging as before commencing 1/4in (1cm) beyond the point where the free i-cord began. When you have reached the top of the opening, break off the yarn leaving a short tail and finish as at the top of the mitten.

FINISHING

In order to show off the lace pattern, soak the gloves and pin each out to form a rectangle 9in (23cm) long and 7 (8:9) cm (2 3/4in) wide. ⊕

CASATI CARDIGAN
& GLOVES

DULCIE
TUNIC

SPRITE
DRESS

MULLIGAN
STOLE

CLARISSA
CARDIGAN

Light lace

Amanda Jones
Dulcie Tunic

Lightweight lace top uses a lovely shell pattern
on the waist, sleeves and central panel

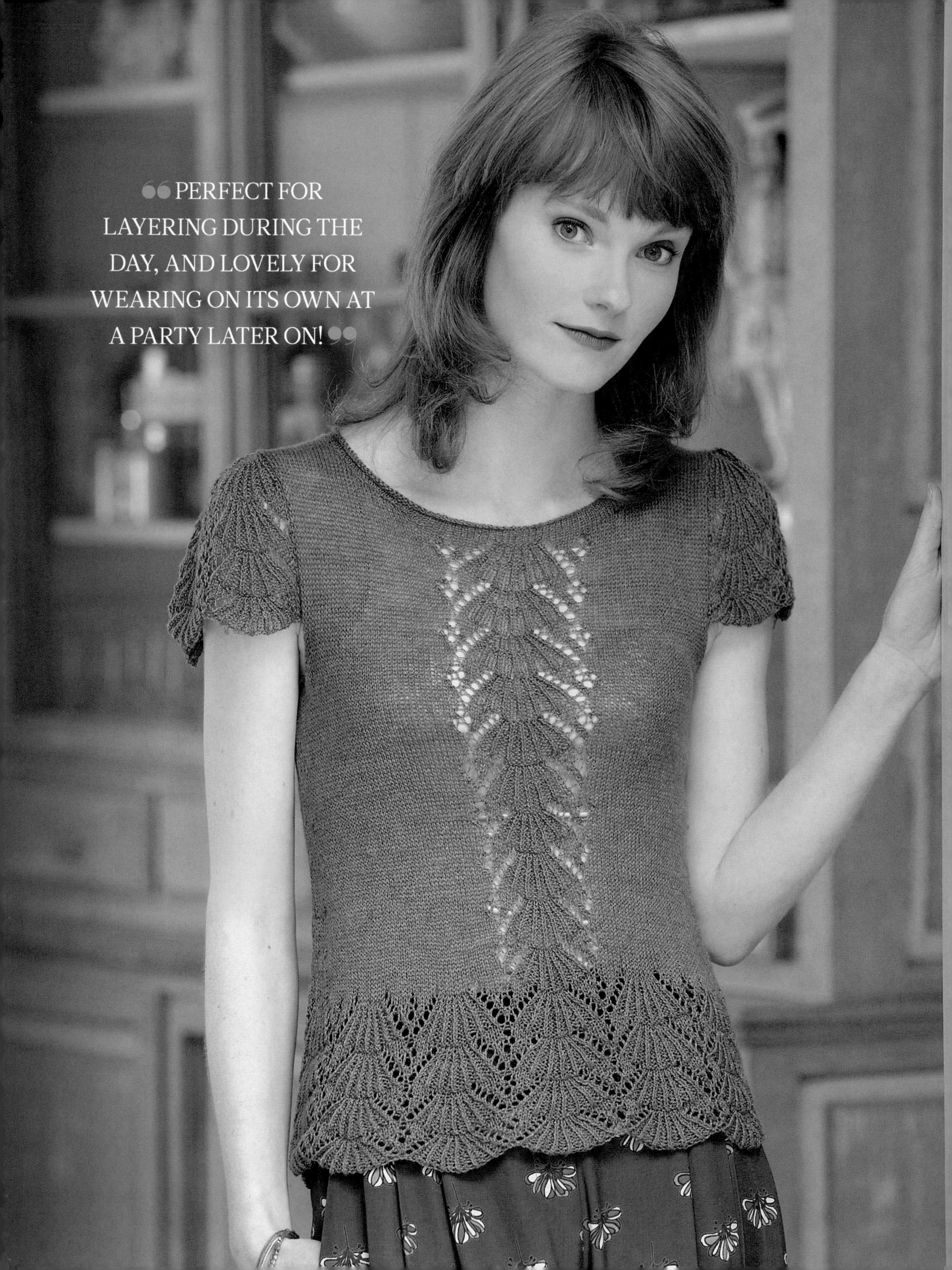

“PERFECT FOR LAYERING DURING THE DAY, AND LOVELY FOR WEARING ON ITS OWN AT A PARTY LATER ON!”

SIZE

		6	8	10	12	14	16	18	20	
TO FIT BUST		76	81	86	91	97	102	107	112	cm
		30	32	34	36	38	40	42	44	in
ACTUAL BUST		76	81	84½	89	95	101	109½	112½	cm
		30	32	33¼	35	37½	39½	43	44½	in
ACTUAL LENGTH		53	53	53	57	57	58	59	60	cm
		21	21	21	22½	22½	23	23¼	23½	in
SLEEVE SEAM		12¼	12¼	12¼	15½	15½	15½	15½	15½	cm
		4¾	4¾	4¾	6	6	6	6	6	in

YARN

This project was stitched with **Fyberspates** Scrumptious Lace, lace weight (45% silk, 55% merino wool); 3½oz/100g, 1,094yds/1,000m

	6	8	10	12	14	16	18	20	
ROSE PINK (509)	1	1	1	2	2	2	2	2	x100g skeins

Amanda Jones
Dulcie Tunic

THIS LITTLE top by Amanda Jones has a pretty shell-like edging and sleeves, and is knitted in a fine lace weight yarn, making it a perfect layering item for day, and a lovely option for wearing on its own at an evening celebration. It would be a pretty knit for a teenager as well as an adult, so we have provided a generous range of UK sizes, starting at a size 6 and going up to a 20.

BODY

Using 3.5mm circular needles, cast on 240 (240:240:280:280:280:320:320) sts. Join to work in the round, being careful not to twist work. Place marker at beg of rnd. Knit 1 round.

LACE BORDER PATTERN

Lace is worked over 20 sts per repeat. We advise marking each repeat with stitch markers and have included the st counts per repeat for each time there is an increase or decrease, to help you keep track.
Rnd 1: *K1, yo, (K1b, P2) 6 times, K1b, yo; rep from * to end. 22 sts per repeat.
Rnd 2: *K2, (K1b, P2) 6 times, K1b, K1; rep from * to end.
Rnd 3: *K2, yo, (K1b, P2) 6 times, K1b, yo, K1; rep from * to end. 24 sts per repeat
Rnd 4: *K3, (K1b, P2) 6 times, K1b, K2; rep from * to end.
Rnd 5: *Yo, K2tog, K1, yo, (K1b, P2) 6 times, K1b, yo, K2; rep from * to end. 26 sts per repeat.
Rnd 6: *K4, (K1b, P2) 6 times, K1b, K3; rep from * to end.

Rnd 7: *K1, yo, skpo, K1, yo, (K1b, P2tog) 6 times, K1b, yo, K1, K2tog, yo; rep from * to end. 22 sts per repeat.
Rnd 8: *K5, (K1b, P1) 6 times, K1b, K4; rep from * to end.
Rnd 9: *Yo, K2tog, K3, yo, (K1b, P1) 6 times, K1b, yo, K4; rep from * to end. 24 sts per repeat.
Rnd 10: *K6, (K1b, P1) 6 times, K1b, K5; rep from * to end.
Rnd 11: *K6, yo, (K2tog tbl) 3 times, K1b, (K2tog) 3 times, yo, K5; rep from * to end. 20 sts per repeat.
Rnd 12: *K7, P7, K6; rep from * to end. Working from Border Chart or written instructions above, rep Rnds 1 to 12 four times in total.

Sizes 6, 8, 10, 18 & 20 only
Break yarn, slip next 10 sts to right needle, pm and rejoin yarn. This is the left side.

All sizes
You will now work side shaping over front and back sections in st st in the round while continuing a lace central panel which is worked over 19 sts.

LACE CENTRAL PANEL PATTERN
Rnd 1 (RS): Yo, (K1b, P2) 6 times, K1b, yo. 21 sts for central panel.
Rnd 2 (WS): K1, (K1b, P2) 6 times, K1b, K1.
Rnd 3: K1, yo, (K1b, P2) 6 times, K1b, yo, K1. 23 sts for central panel.
Rnd 4: K2, (K1b, P2) 6 times, K1b, K2.
Rnd 5: K2, yo (K1b, P2) 6 times, K1b, yo, K2. 25 sts for central panel.
Rnd 6: K3, (K1b, P2) 6 times, K1b, K3.

Rnd 7: K3, yo, (K1b, P2tog) 6 times, K1b, yo, K3. 21 sts for central panel.
Rnd 8: K4, (K1b, P1) 6 times, K1b, K4.
Rnd 9: K4, yo, (K1b, P1) 6 times, K1b, yo, K4. 23 sts for central panel.
Rnd 10: K5, (K1b, P1) 6 times, K1b, K5.
Rnd 11: K5, yo, (K2tog tbl) 3 times, K1b, (K2tog) 3 times, yo, K5. 19 sts for central panel.
Rnd 12: K6, P7, K6.

BEGIN SIDE SHAPING
Rnd 1: K1, skpo, K48 (48:48:58:58:58:68:68), place 1st marker, work Rnd 1 of lace central panel, place 2nd marker, K48 (18:48:58:58:58:68:68), K2tog, K1, place 3rd marker, K1, skpo, K to 3 sts before last marker, K2tog, K1.
121 (121:121:141:141:141:161:161) sts for front.
117 (117:117:137:137:137:157:157) sts for back. Total 238 (238:238:278:278:318:318:318) sts.

This sets the position for the central panel and for the front and side seams. Not counting increases or decreases for the front lace panel (Rnd 1 has 2 lace increases), the Front has 2 more sts than the Back.

Cont working from Rnd 2 of lace patt from Central Panel chart or written instructions above, and st st for the back section as set. AT THE SAME TIME work side shaping as foll:
On foll 8th (12th:24th:8th:12th:24th:8th:12th) round, *K1, skpo, patt to 3 sts before side marker, K2tog, K1; rep from * to end. Dec as set on every foll 8th (12th:24th:8th:12th:24th:8th:12th) round until 103 (111:

NEEDLES & ACCESSORIES

1 set 3.5mm (UK 9-10/US 4) circular needles, 31½in (80cm) long
1 set 3mm (UK 11/US 2-3) circular needles, 50cm long
1 pair 3.5mm (UK 9-10/US 4) knitting needles
4 stitch markers

GAUGE

27 sts and 39 rows to 4in (10cm) measured over st st on 3.5mm needles

SPECIAL ABBREVIATIONS

K1b: knit into back of stitch.
P1b: purl into back of stitch.
skpo: slip 1 st, knit 1 st, pass slipped st over.

NOTES

This garment is knitted in the round until the armholes.
When working from charts in the round, read all rounds from right to left.
When working from charts flat read all odd number (RS) rows from right to left and all even number (WS) rows from left to right.

Use stitch markers for the sides, centered at the underarm and to mark either side of the central lace pattern.
All side shaping is worked around the stitch markers.

BLOCKING DIAGRAM

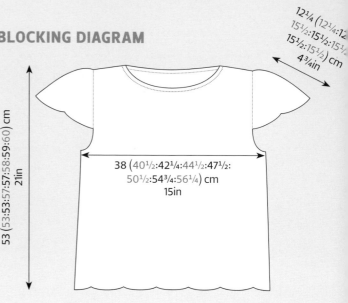

12¼ (12¼:12¼:15½:15½:15½:15½) cm
4¾in

53 (53:53:57:57:58:59:60) cm
21in

38 (40½:42¼:44½:47½: 50½:54¾:56¼) cm
15in

115:121:129:137:149:153) sts rem in front section and 101 (109:113:119:127:135:147:151) sts rem in back section [counted after 12th round has been worked]. If counting after the final dec round you would have 109 (113:117:123:131:139:155:155) sts at the end of that round for the front. The back st count would be the same as given above.
Total 204 (220:228:240:256:272:296:304) sts.
Cont without shaping until you have completed 11 (11:11:12:12:12:12:12) full patt reps of central lace panel (starting from cast on edge), ending on the 12th round.

DIVIDE FOR ARMHOLES AND FRONT SECTION

Next row (RS): Cont to work lace central panel FLAT as set from Central Panel chart, or written instructions below, starting at Row 1, cast off 6 (6:6:6:6:7:7) sts, patt across to side marker, turn, leave rem sts on circular needle or waste yarn for back.

CENTRAL LACE PANEL WORKED FLAT

Row 1 (RS): Yo, (K1b, P2) 6 times, K1b, yo. 21 sts for central panel.
Row 2 (WS): P1, (P1b, K2) 6 times, P1b, P1.
Row 3: K1, yo, (K1b, P2) 6 times, K1b, yo, K1. 23 sts for central panel.
Row 4: P2, (P1b, K2) 6 times, P1b, P2.
Row 5: K2, yo (K1b, P2) 6 times, K1b, yo, K2. 25sts for central panel.
Row 6: P3, (P1b, K2) 6 times, P1b, P3.
Row 7: K3, yo, (K1b, P2tog) 6 times, K1b, yo, K3. 21 sts for central panel.
Row 8: P4, (P1b, K1) 6 times, P1b, P4.
Row 9: K4, yo, (K1b, P1) 6 times, K1b, yo, K4. 23 sts for central panel.
Row 10: P5, (P1b, K1) 6 times, P1b, P5.

Row 11: K5, yo, (K2tog tbl) 3 times, K1b, (K2tog) 3 times, yo, K5. 19 sts for central panel.
Row 12: P6, K7, P6.

FRONT

Keeping central lace panel correct, cast off 6 (6:6:6:6:7:7) sts at beg of row. 93 (101:105:111:119:127:137:141) sts. This st count includes the inc of 2 sts within lace panel. Dec 1 st at each end of the next 3 rows. 89 (97:101:107:115:123:133:137) sts rem, including extra sts within panel. After Row 12 of pattern there will be 85 (93:97:103:111:119:129:133) sts.

Cont without shaping until you have completed 14 (14:14:14:15:15:15:15) full patt reps ending on 12th row (WS).

FRONT NECK SHAPING

Next row (RS): K across 30 (32:34:33:35:38: 42:44) sts, turn, leave rem sts on a spare needle and work each side separately.
Next row: (WS): Cast off 4 sts at beg of next row, then dec 1 st at neck edge of every foll row until 23 (24:25:26:29:31:32:34) sts rem. Cont to dec at neck edge on every foll alt row until 18 (20:21:21:23:24:25:26) sts rem. Cont without shaping until armhole meas 19 (19:19:20:20:21:22:23) cm from beg of armhole shaping, ending on a WS row. Break yarn and leave sts on a holder to cast off with the back later.

With RS facing slip center 25 (29:29:37:41: 43:45:45) sts onto a holder for the front neck. Rejoin yarn and knit to end of row.

Next row (WS): Dec 1 st at end of next row.
Next row (RS): Cast off 4 sts at beg of row. Complete to match first side, reversing shapings. Leave rem sts on a holder.

BACK

With RS facing re-join yarn to back section. Cast off 6 (6:6:6:6:7:7) sts at the beg of the next 2 rows.
89 (97:101:107:115:123:133:137) sts.
Then dec 1 st at each end of the next 3 (3:4:5:5:5:5:5) rows.
83 (91:93:97:105:113:123:127) sts.
Cont without shaping until the armhole meas 17 (17:17:18:18:19:20:21) cm from beg of armhole shaping, ending on a WS row.

BACK NECK SHAPING

Next row (RS): K across 27 (28:29:28: 30:31:33:34), turn, leave rem sts on a spare needle and work each side separately.
Next row (WS): Cast off 4 sts and dec 1 st (both at neck edge), work to end of row.
22 (23:24:23:25:26:28:29) sts.
Dec 1 st at neck edge of the next 4 (3:3:2:2:2:3:3) rows.
18 (20:21:21:23:24:25:26) sts.
Work 0 (1:1:2:2:3:1:1) rows straight.
The front will be very slightly longer than the back, so that when you join the shoulders the seam will lie more comfortably, just behind the top of the shoulder.

With RS facing slip center 29 (35:35:41:45: 53:57:59) sts to a holder for the back neck. Rejoin yarn and knit to end of row.
Complete to match first side. ▶

SLEEVE CHART

CENTRAL PANEL CHART

BORDER CHART

KEY

- ☐ K on RS, P on WS
- ● P on RS, K on WS
- ○ yo
- ⟋ K2tog
- ⤫ K2tog tbl
- ⟍ skpo
- ⟋ P2tog
- ⤫ K1tbl on RS, P1tbl on WS
- ▨ No stitch
- ☐ Pattern repeat

FINISHING

With RS of front facing RS of back, cast off each front shoulder with the corresponding back shoulder using the three-needle cast-off method.

SLEEVES (Work 2 alike)

Lace pattern for the sleeves is worked flat as a multiple of 20 +1 as foll:

Row 1 (RS): *K1, yo, (K1b, P2) 6 times, K1b, yo; rep from * to last st, K1. 22sts per rep +1.
Row 2 (WS): P1 *P1, (P1b, K2) 6 times, P1b, P2; rep from * to end.
Row 3: *K2, yo, (K1b, P2) 6 times, K1b, yo, K1; rep from * to last st, K1. 24sts per rep +1.
Row 4: P1 *P2, (P1b, K2) 6 times, P1b, P3; rep from * to end.
Row 5: K3, yo (K1b, P2) 6 times, K1b, yo, K2, *yo, K2tog, K1, yo (K1b, P2) 6 times, K1b, yo, K2; rep from * to last st, K1. 26sts per rep +1.
Row 6: P1 *P3, (P1b, K2) 6 times, P1b, P4; rep from * to end.
Row 7: *K1, yo, skpo, K1, yo, (K1b, P2tog) 6 times, K1b, yo, K1, K2tog, yo; rep from * to last st, K1. 22 sts per rep +1.
Row 8: P1 *P4, (P1b, K1) 6 times, P1b, P5.
Row 9: K5, (K1b, P1) 6 times, K1b, yo, K4, *yo, skpo, K3, yo, (K1b, P1) 6 times, K1b, yo, K4; rep from * to last st, K1. 24sts per rep +1
Row 10: P1 *P5, (P1b, K1) 6 times, P1b, P5; rep from * to end.
Row 11: *K6, yo, (K2tog tbl) 3 times, K1b, (K2tog) 3 times, yo, K5; rep from * to last st, K1. 20 sts per rep +1.
Row 12: P1 *P6, K7, P6; rep from * to end.

Using 3.5mm needles cast on 81 (81:101: 101:121:121:121:121) sts.
Work border patt flat from Sleeves chart or written instructions above until you have completed 3 (3:3:4:4:4:4:4) full patt reps, ending on Row 12 (WS).

SHAPE SLEEVE TOP

Cont in patt as before but DO NOT WORK incs and decs at beg and end of rows. Instead, beg and end all RS rows with K1, and WS rows with P1, as foll:
Row 1: K1, (K1b, P2) 6 times, K1b, yo, *K1, yo, (K1b, P2) 6 times, K1b, yo; rep from *, ending last rep, K1, yo, (K1b, P2,) 6 times, K1b, K1.
Row 2 (WS): P1, (P1b, K2) 6 times, P1b, P2, *P1, (P1b, K2) 6 times, P1b, P2; rep from *, ending last rep, P1, (P1b, K2) 6 times, P1b, P1.
Row 3: K1, (K1b, P2) 6 times, K1b, yo, K1, *K2, yo, (K1b, P2) 6 times, K1b, yo, K1; rep from *, ending last rep, K2, yo, (K1b, P2) 6 times, K1b, K1.

Cont as set until all 12 rows of lace pattern have been worked in this manner once. Cast off knitwise.

NECKBAND

With RS facing, using 3mm circular needles, start at the left shoulder, pick up and knit 37 (37:42:42:45:47:52:52) sts evenly down to the front neck, knit across 25 (29:29:37:41:43:45:45) sts on front neck holder, pick up and knit 37 (37:42:42:45: 47:52:52) sts up to right shoulder, pick up and knit 13 sts down to back neck, knit across 29 (35:35:41:45:53:57:59) sts from back neck holder, pick up and knit 13 sts to left shoulder.
154 (164:174:188:202:216:232:234) sts, place marker and join to work in the round.

Work 8 rounds in st st. Cast off using a stretchy cast-off, such as the sewn cast-off method.

SEWN CAST OFF METHOD

Break yarn approx 3 times the length of the edge to cast off and thread onto tapestry needle. *pass yarn through first 2 sts on LH needle from right to left. Then pass it back over the second st and through the first st and slip first st off needle. Rep from * to last st and fasten off.

FINISHING

Block gently according to any yarn care instructions on the yarn label.
With double thread, work a row of running st across the top cast off edge of the sleeve. Pull through evenly to gather until the sleeve top measures 10 (10:10:10:12:12:12:12) cm (4in) and fasten off securely.
Place a pin 5 (5:5:5:6:6:6:6) cm (2in) down from the shoulder seam on the front and back. Pin the gathered edge of the sleeve top, matching the center of the sleeve to the shoulder seam and sew in place, continue to sew the shaped edge and the side edge of the sleeve to the armhole on both sides. Block lightly.
Sew in all ends. ⊕

Sarah Hatton

Casati Cardigan & Gloves

Add some Hollywood glamour with this elegant eveningwear
set, knitted in gorgeous kid mohair and silk blend yarn

Casati Cardigan

SIZE

	8	10	12	14	16	18	20	22	
TO FIT BUST	81	86	91	96	101	107	112	117	cm
	32	34	36	38	40	42	44	46	in
ACTUAL BUST	86	92	96	101	106	112	118	124	cm
	34	35	37	40	42	44	46	49	in
ACTUAL LENGTH	43	43	44	46	46	48	48	50	cm
	17	17	17¼	18	18	19	19	19½	in
SLEEVE SEAM	6	6	6	6	6	6	6	6	cm
	2½	2½	2½	2½	2½	2½	2½	2½	in

YARN

This project was stitched with the following yarns.
Anchor Artiste Metallic, (US: fingering) (80% viscose, 20% metallized polyester); ⅞oz/25g, 109yds/100m

A PEWTER (324)	1	1	1	1	1	1	1	1	x25g BALLS

Rowan Kidsilk Haze, (US: lace weight) (70% super kid mohair, 30% silk); ⅞oz/25g, 230yds/210m

B SMOKE (605)	4	4	5	5	6	6	6	7	x25g BALLS

NEEDLES & ACCESSORIES

1 set 2.75mm (UK 12/US 2) circular needles
1 set 3mm (UK 11/US 3) circular needles
1 pair 3mm (UK 11/US 3) knitting needles
Hook and eyes fastening or press stud fastening

GAUGE

28 sts and 38 rows to 4in (10cm) measured over st st using 3mm needles

---

DRESS TO impress in Sarah Hatton's flattering short-sleeved cardigan with lace details. The gloves will bring glamour to a formal outfit, but would be a charming addition to any wardrobe.

Made from 70% super kid mohair and 30% silk, Rowan's Kidsilk Haze is a beautiful yarn and the ideal complement to this set. "I wanted something feminine and elegant, and felt the Kidsilk Haze and metallic combination was perfect for this – especially in the glamorous grey colorway," says Sarah.

BODY

(worked in one piece to armholes)
**Using 3mm needle and yarn A cast on 243 (255:267:279:303:315:327:351) sts.
Change to yarn B and cont as folls:
Row 1 (RS): K2, *yfwd, K4, Sl 1, K2tog, psso, K4, yfwd, K1; rep from * to last st, K1.
Row 2 and every foll alt row: Purl.
Row 3: K2, *K1, yfwd, K3, Sl 1, K2tog, psso, K3, yfwd, K2; rep from * to last st, K1.
Row 5: K2, *K2, yfwd, K2, Sl 1, K2tog, psso, K2, yfwd, K3; rep from * to last st, K1.
Row 7: K2, *K3, yfwd, K1, Sl 1, K2tog, psso, K1, yfwd, K4; rep from * to last st, K1.
Row 9: K2, *K4, yfwd, Sl 1, K2tog, psso, yfwd, K5; rep from * to last st, K1.
Row 10: Purl.
These 10 rows set lace patt. **
Rep these 10 rows 5 times more.

Leave these sts on a spare needle. Break off yarn.

Make another piece by repeating from ** to **.
Rep these 10 rows 3 times more.
Holding this needle in front of spare needle, knit across row working one stitch from each needle together at the same time to join.
Next row (WS): Purl.
Leave these sts on a spare needle. Break off yarn.
Make a third piece by repeating from ** to **.
Rep these 10 rows once more.
Holding this needle in front of spare needle, knit across row working one stitch from each needle together at the same time to join.

Beg with a purl row, cont in st st until piece meas 23 (23:23:25:24:26:25:27) cm, ending with RS facing for next row.

SHAPE ARMHOLES

Next row: K56 (58:60:62:68:71:73:79), cast off 10 (12:14:16:16:16:18:18) sts loosely, knit until there are 111 (115:119:123:135:141:145:157) sts on needle after cast-off sts, cast off 10 (12:14:16:16:16:18:18) sts loosely, knit to end.
Next row (WS): Purl until there are 56 (58:60:62:68:71:73:79) sts on needle, turn, leave rem sts on a holder and cont on these sts only.

SHAPE LEFT FRONT

Dec 1 st at beg (armhole edge) of next and 6 (6:6:6:10:12:12:16) foll rows, then on 2 (3:3:3:3:2:2:2) foll alt rows AT SAME TIME dec 1 st at end (neck edge) of next and 5 (6:6:6:7:7:8:10) foll alt rows.
41 (41:43:45:46:48:49:49) sts.

Dec 1 st at neck edge only in 2nd and 10 (10:6:6:8:8:7:5) foll alt rows, then on every foll 4th row to 23 (24:26:28:28:30:32:34) sts.
Cont until armhole meas 20 (20:21:21:22:22:23:23) cm, ending with WS facing for next row.

SHAPE SHOULDER

Next row (RS): Cast off 11 (12:13:14:14:15:16:17) sts loosely, knit to end.
Work 1 row.
Cast off rem 12 (12:13:14:14:15:16:17) sts loosely.

BACK

With WS facing, rejoin yarn to center 111 (115:119:123:135:141:145:157) sts, purl to end.

SHAPE ARMHOLES

Dec 1 st at each end of next 7 (7:7:7:11:13:13:17) rows, then on 2 (3:3:3:3:2:2:2) foll alt

BLOCKING DIAGRAM

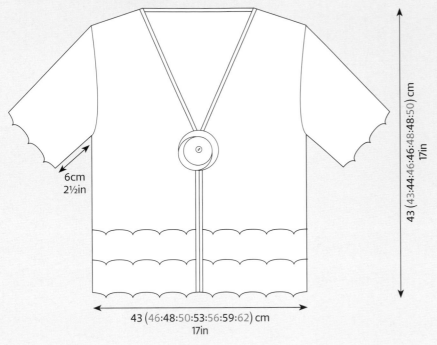

6cm
2½in

43 (43:44:44:46:46:48:48:50) cm
17in

43 (46:48:50:53:56:59:62) cm
17in

FINISHING

Block gently as described on the ball band. Join both shoulder seams, using back stitch, or mattress stitch if preferred.

NECKBAND

With RS facing, using 2.75mm needle and yarn B, pick up and knit 75 (75:75:82:79:85:82:89) sts evenly up right front to start of neck shaping, 66 (66:69:69:73:73:76:76) sts evenly along shaped edge, 47 (47:47:47:51:51:51:51) sts from back neck, 66 (66:69:69:73:73:76:76) sts evenly along shaped edge and 75 (75:75:82:79:85:82:89) sts evenly down left front to cast-on edge.
329 (329:335:349:355:367:367:381) sts.
Knit 4 rows.
Cast off knitwise loosely on WS.

CORSAGE

Using 3mm needles and yarn A cast on 50 sts.
Change to yarn B and beg with a knit row, work 4 rows in st st.
Next row: *K5, K2tog; rep from * to last st, K1.
Work 3 rows in st st.
Next row: *K4, K2tog; rep from * to last st, K1.
Work 1 row in st st.
Next row: *K3, K2tog; rep from * to last st, K1.
Work 1 row in st st.
Next row: *K2, K2tog; rep from * to last st, K1.
Work 1 row in st st.
Next row: *K1, K2tog; rep from * to last st, K1.
Work 1 row in st st.
Cast off.

Run gathering stitch along cast-off row and gather slightly. Sew into a flower-like shape.
Sew press stud or hook and eye to front edges, just below start of neck shaping, and sew corsage in place on top of the fastening.
Join sleeve seams and sew sleeves in place. ▶

rows. 93 (95:99:103:107:111:115:119) sts.

Cont without shaping until armhole meas 20 (20:21:21:22:22:23:23)cm, ending with RS facing for next row.

SHAPE SHOULDERS
Next row (RS): Cast off 11 (12:13:14:14:15:16:17) sts loosely, knit until there are 16 (16:17:18:18:19:20:21) sts on right needle and turn, leaving rem sts on a holder.

Next row (WS): Cast off 4 sts loosely, purl to end.
Cast off rem 12 (12:13:14:14:15:16:17) sts loosely.
With RS facing, rejoin yarn to rem sts, cast off center 39 (39:39:39:43:43:43:43) sts loosely, knit to end.
Complete to match first side, reversing all shapings.

RIGHT FRONT

With RS facing, rejoin yarn to rem 56 (58:60:62:68:71:73:79) sts, purl to end.

Complete to match Left Front reversing all shapings.

SLEEVES (make 2)
Using 3mm needle and yarn A cast on 89 (97:101:107:107:113:117:123) sts.
Change to yarn B and cont as folls:
**Row 1 (RS): K3 (1:3:6:6:3:5:2), *yfwd, K4,

Sl1, K2tog, psso, K4, yfwd, K1; rep from * to last 2 (0:2:5:5:2:4:1) sts, K2 (0:2:5:5:2:4:1).
Row 2 and every foll alt row: Purl.
Row 3: K3 (1:3:6:6:3:5:2), *K1, yfwd, K3, Sl1, K2tog, K3, yfwd, K2; rep from * to last 2 (0:2:5:5:2:4:1) sts, K2 (0:2:5:5:2:4:1).
Row 5: K3 (1:3:6:6:3:5:2), *K2, yfwd, K2, Sl1, K2tog, psso, K2, yfwd, K3; rep from * to last 2 (0:2:5:5:2:4:1) sts, K2 (0:2:5:5:2:4:1).
Row 7: K3 (1:3:6:6:3:5:2), *K3, yfwd, K1, Sl1, K2tog, psso, K1, yfwd, K4; rep from * to last 2 (0:2:5:5:2:4:1) sts, K2 (0:2:5:5:2:4:1).
Row 9: K3 (1:3:6:6:3:5:2), *K4, yfwd, Sl1, K2tog, psso, yfwd, K5; rep from * to last 2 (0:2:5:5:2:4:1) sts, K2 (0:2:5:5:2:4:1).
Row 10: Purl.

Beg with a purl row, work 3 rows in st st, ending with RS facing for next row.

SHAPE SLEEVEHEAD
Cast off 5 (6:7:8:8:8:9:9) sts loosely at beg of next 2 rows. 79 (85:87:91:91:97:99:105) sts.
Dec 1 st at each end of next 10 (10:12:12:12:12:12:12) rows.
59 (65:63:67:67:73:75:81) sts.
Dec 1 st at each end of next and every foll alt row to 43 (47:47:47:47:43:47:51) sts.
Work 1 row straight.
Dec 1 st at each end of every row 8 (10:10:10:10:8:10:12) times. 27 sts.
Cast off 7 sts loosely at beg of next 2 rows. 13 sts.
Cast off rem 13 sts loosely.

Decreases and increases in the lace pattern create the scalloped edging

Casati Gloves

Sarah Hatton
Casati Gloves

SIZE

To fit average adult woman's hand.

YARN

This project was stitched with the following yarns.
Anchor Artiste Metallic, (US: fingering) (80% viscose, 20% metallized polyester); ⅞oz/25g, 109yds/100m
A Pewter (324) 1 x 25g ball
Rowan Kidsilk Haze, (US: lace weight) (70% super kid mohair, 30% silk); ⅞oz/25g, 230yds/210m
B Smoke (605) 1 x 25g ball

NEEDLES & ACCESSORIES

1 pair 2.75mm (UK 12/US 2) knitting needles
1 pair 3mm (UK 11/ US 3) knitting needles
Spare needle

GAUGE

32 sts and 42 rows to 10cm over st st using 2.75mm needles

RIGHT GLOVE

Using 3mm needles and yarn A cast on 63 sts.
Change to yarn B and cont as folls:
Row 1 (RS): K2, *yfwd, K4, Sl 1, K2tog, psso, K4, yfwd, K1;, rep from * to last st, K1.
Row 2 and every foll alt row: Purl.
Row 3: K2, *K1, yfwd, K3, Sl 1, K2tog, psso, K3, yfwd, K2; rep from * to last st, K1.
Row 5: K2, *K2, yfwd, K2, Sl 1, K2tog, psso, K2, yfwd, K3; rep from * to last st, K1.
Row 7: K2, *K3, yfwd, K1, Sl 1, K2tog, psso, K1, yfwd, K4; rep from * to last st, K1.
Row 9: K2, *K4, yfwd, Sl 1, K2tog, psso, yfwd, K5; rep from * to last st, K1.
Row 10: Purl.
These 10 rows set lace patt. Work another 10 rows in patt as set.
Leave these sts on a spare needle.

Using 3mm needles and yarn A cast on 63 sts.
Change to yarn B and work 10 rows in lace patt as set.
Holding this piece of work in front of piece on spare needle, knit across row working one stitch from each needle together at the same time to join.

Change to 2.75mm needles.
Beg with a purl row, working in st st throughout, dec 1 st at each end of 2nd and 4 foll 6th rows. 53 sts.
Work 13 rows without shaping, inc 1 st at end of last row. **

SHAPE THUMB

Row 1 (RS): K28, KFB, K2, KFB, K22.
Work 3 rows.

Row 5: K28, KFB, K4, KFB, K22. 58 sts.
Work 3 rows.
Cont in this way, increasing 2 sts on next and every foll 4th row until there are 68 sts.
Work 3 rows, ending with RS facing for next row.
Next row (RS): K46, turn and cast on 2 sts.
Next row: P20, turn and cast on 2 sts.
*** Cont on these 22 sts until work meas 6cm from cast-on sts, ending with RS facing for next row.

Next row (RS): (K2tog, K2) 5 times, K2. 17 sts.
Work 1 row.
Next row: (K2tog) 8 times, K1.
Break yarn and thread through rem sts.
Fasten off tightly then join seam. Thumb is now formed.

With RS facing, rejoin yarn and pick up and knit 6 sts from base of thumb, knit to end. 56 sts.
Cont without shaping for 4cm, ending with RS facing for next row.

SHAPE FIRST FINGER

Next row (RS): K36, turn and cast on 1 st.
Next row: P17, turn and cast on 1 st.
Working on these 18 sts only, cont without shaping for 7cm, ending with RS facing for next row.
Next row (RS): (K2tog, K2) 4 times, K2. 14 sts.
Work 1 row.
Next row: (K2tog) 7 times.
Break yarn and thread through rem sts.
Fasten off tightly then join seam.

SHAPE SECOND FINGER

With RS facing, rejoin yarn and pick up and knit 2 sts from base of first finger, K7, turn and cast on 1 st.
Next row (WS): P17, turn and cast on 1 st.
Working on these 18 sts only, cont without

Like the cardigan, each glove is finished with a corsage – we've attached them using a 10mm button

shaping for 8cm, ending with RS facing
for next row.
Next row (RS): (K2tog, K2) 4 times, K2.
14 sts.
Work 1 row.
Next row: (K2tog) 7 times.
Break yarn and thread through rem sts.
Fasten off tightly then join seam.

SHAPE THIRD FINGER

With RS facing, rejoin yarn and pick up
and knit 2 sts from base of second finger,
K7, turn and cast on 1 st.
Next row (WS): P17, turn and cast on 1 st.
Working on these 18 sts only, cont without
shaping for 7cm, ending with RS facing for
next row.
Next row (RS): (K2tog, K2) 4 times, K2.
14 sts.
Work 1 row.
Next row: (K2tog) 7 times.
Break yarn and thread through rem sts.
Fasten off tightly then join seam.

SHAPE FOURTH FINGER

With RS facing, rejoin yarn and pick up
and knit 4 sts from base of third finger,
knit to end.
Next row: P16.
Working on these 16 sts, cont without
shaping for 6cm, ending with RS facing
for next row.
Next row (RS): (K2tog, K2) 4 times. 12 sts.
Work 1 row.
Next row: (K2tog) 6 times.
Break yarn and thread through rem sts.
Fasten off tightly and join finger and
side seam.

LEFT GLOVE

Work as given for right glove to **.

SHAPE THUMB

Row 1 (RS): K22, KFB, K2, KFB, K28.
Work 3 rows.
Row 5: K22, KFB, K6, KFB, K28. 58 sts.
Work 3 rows.
Cont in this way, increasing 2 sts on next
and every foll 4th row until there are 68 sts.

Work 3 rows, ending with RS facing for
next row.
Next row (RS): K40, turn and cast on 2 sts.
Next row: P20, turn and cast on 2 sts.
Complete as given for right glove from ***.

CORSAGE

Make two corsages following the
instructions given for the Cardigan. Sew
corsage onto each glove as desired. ⊕

The Artiste
Metallic yarn adds
highlights along
the front frills and
sleeve edgings

Jean Moss
Sprite Dress

As fabulous to knit as it is to wear, this asymmetric dress
features a fishscale lace pattern and scattered flowers

“THE SLASHED NECKLINE AND CAP SLEEVES ADD VERSATILITY – WEAR IT WITH ANYTHING!”

Jean Moss
Sprite Dress

THE STUNNING designs of Jean Moss have won her many fans, and this creation is typically eye-catching. Named Sprite, it's sure to impress with its asymmetric shape, lace pattern and flowers at the neck, waist and hem.

Jean says: "I've always loved the work of Arthur Rackham, and wanted Sprite to be a piece that was at home in his supernatural illustrations. The fashions of the 1930s were also a big influence, so I gave the design a dropped waist. The slashed neckline and cap sleeves add versatility; wear it with a long-sleeved top, strappy camisole or nothing at all!"

Jean adds: "The gorgeous Siena yarn gives a crisp definition to the stitch patterns and the final touch was the sprinkling of flowers - everything you need to take you away with the fairies!"

SIZE

		XS	S	M	L	XL	
TO FIT BUST		81	86	91	96	101	cm
		32	34	36	38½	40	in
ACTUAL BUST		84	89	94	99	104	cm
		33	35	37	39	41	in
ACTUAL LENGTH		99	99	100½	101½	101½	cm
		39	39	39½	40	40	in

YARN

This project was stitched with **Rowan** Siena 4ply, 4ply (US: fingering) (100% mercerized cotton); 1¾oz/50g, 153yds/140m

	XS	S	M	L	XL	
SHADOW (667)	10	11	11	12	13	x50g BALLS

STITCH PATTERNS

FISHSCALE PATTERN
Multiple of 20 + 1 sts and 16 rows.
Row 1(RS): *Yo, K4, Sl1, K2tog, psso, K4, yo, K3, yo, Sl1, K2tog, psso, yo, K3; rep from *, ending K4 (instead of K3).
Row 2 and all even rows: Purl.
Row 3: K1, *yo, K3, Sl1, K2tog, psso, K3, yo, K11; rep from * to end.
Row 5: K1, *K1, yo, K2, Sl1, K2tog, psso, K2, yo, K12; rep from * to end.
Row 7: K1, *K2, yo, K1, Sl1, K2tog, psso, K1, yo, K13; rep from * to end.
Row 9: K1, *K3, yo, Sl1, K2tog, psso, yo, K3, yo, K4, Sl1, K2tog, psso, K4, yo; rep from * to end.
Row 11: K1, *K10, yo, K3, Sl1, K2tog, psso, K3, yo, K1; rep from * to end.
Row 13: K1, *K11, yo, K2, Sl1, K2tog, psso, K2, yo, K2; rep from * to end.
Row 15: K1, *K12, yo, K1, Sl1, K2tog, psso, K1, yo, K3; rep from * to end.
Rep these 16 rows.

SLIP STITCH RIB
Multiple of 4 sts and 2 rows.
Row 1(RS): *K2, yo, Sl1, K1, psso; rep from * to end.
Row 2: *P2, yo, P2tog; rep from * to end.
Rep these 2 rows.

FLOWERS
Make 12 flowers in single thread using 3.5mm needles and make 10 in doubled thread on 4mm needles.
Using larger needles, cast on 10 sts.
Row 1: Knit.
Row 2: KFB to end. 20 sts.
Row 3: Knit.
Row 4: KFB to end. 40 sts.
Row 5: Knit.
Cast off. Twist into rose shape and secure with end of yarn.

FLORETS
Make 12 in single thread using 3.25mm needles.
Cast on 21 sts loosely. Work 3 rows in garter st. Pass all stitches one at a time over first stitch, then fasten off. Turn cast-on edge into cast-off edge making one twist to form floret, then sew into place.

BACK
Using 3.5mm needles, cast on 21 sts and refer to fishscale pattern and repeat the 16 rows working as follows:
XS: Inc 2 sts at end of every alt row 6 times, then inc 4 sts at end of every alt row 22 times. 121 sts.
S & M: Inc 4 sts at end of every alt row

NEEDLES & ACCESSORIES
1 pair 4mm (UK 8/US 6) knitting needles
1 pair 3.5mm (UK 10-9/US 4) knitting needles
1 pair 3.25mm (UK 10/US 3) knitting needles
3.5mm (UK 9/US E4) crochet hook
Stitch holders

GAUGE
24 sts and 32 rows to 4in (10cm) over fishscale patt using 3.5mm needles

ABBREVIATIONS
DC: double crochet (see page 11).
SS: slip st crochet (see page 11).

Crochet edging complements the knitted flowers scattered randomly along the hem, neckline and waist

PATTERN NOTES

Slip the first stitch and knit into the back of the last stitch on every row to make selvage.

BLOCKING DIAGRAM

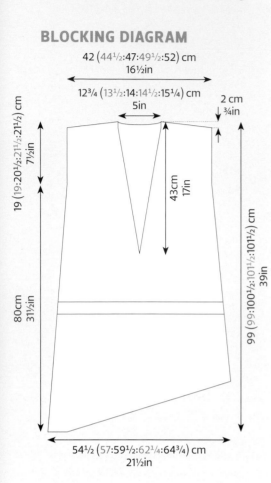

42 (44½:47:49½:52) cm
16½in

12¾ (13½:14:14½:15¼) cm
5in

2 cm
↓ ¾in

19 (19:20½:21½:21½) cm
7½in

43cm
17in

80cm
31½in

99 (99:100½:101½:101½) cm
39in

54½ (57:59½:62¼:64¾) cm
21½in

24 times, then inc 6 sts at end of every alt row 4 times. 141 sts.

L & XL: Inc 4 sts at end of every alt row 14 times, then inc 6 sts at end of every alt row 14 times. 161 sts.

NB: Integrate the extra sts into the fishscale pattern as soon as you have enough sts to do so (every 10 sts increased). When all increases are completed, work should measure 7in (17¾cm) from cast-on edge.

Start decs as follows, keeping fishscale patt correct:

XS: Dec 1 st at both ends of next and every foll 16th row 11 times in all. 99 sts.

S: Dec 1 st at both ends of next and every foll 8th row 5 times in all, then every foll 10th row 13 times. 105 sts.

M: Dec 1 st at both ends of next and every foll 10th row 4 times in all, then every foll 12th row 11 times. 111 sts.

L: Dec 1 st at both ends of next and every foll 6th row 4 times in all, then every foll 8th row 18 times. 117 sts.

▶

Fishscale pattern combines with a slip-stitch rib to give a beautiful texture

Sprite Dress

Floral embellishments are created by twisting knitted lengths into rose shapes

XL: Dec 1 st at both ends of next and every foll 8th row 10 times in all, then every foll 10th row 9 times. 123 sts.

AT THE SAME TIME when work measures 15in (35cm) from cast-on edge, ending on either row 8 or 16 of patt, suspend decreases (making a note of where you are so you can continue after rib) and change to 3.25mm needles. Work 5cm in slip stitch rib, starting on RS row. If your stitch count is not a multiple of four, work extra st in st st at one or both ends, depending on whether there are 1, 2 or 3 extra sts. When rib is completed, change to 3.5mm needles and cont in fishtail patt to end, cont patt from where you left off before rib and keeping dec rows correct.

Work until piece meas 97¼ (97¼:98½: 99¾:99¾) cm (38¼in) ending on WS row.

SHAPE SHOULDERS

Place 11 (12:13:13:14) sts at armhole on holder on next 2 rows, keeping patt correct as set.

Next row (RS): Place 12 (12:13:14:15) sts at armhole edge on holder, work 13 (14:14: 15:16) sts in patt as set, cast off 27 (29:31:33: 33) sts for neck, place rem sts on holder. Rejoin yarn to rem sts and cont as folls:

Next row (WS): Work in patt as set, dec 1 st at neck edge.

Next row (RS): Cast off over all 35 (37:39: 41:44) sts.

Work second side in patt as for first side, reversing shapings.

FRONT

NB: At hem, Front is a mirror image of Back (not identical), so work incs at beg of each row instead of at the end.

Work as for Back, until piece measures 56 (56:57¼: 58½:58½) cm (22in) from cast-on edge, ending on RS row, then shape neckline.

Next row (WS): Work in patt to center st, then place this st and rem sts on holder. Working sides separately, work 1 row in patt, then keeping patt correct as set, dec as folls:

XS: 1 st at neck edge on next and every foll 10th row 11 times in all, then every 8th row 3 times. 35 sts.

S: 1 st at neck edge on next and every foll 10th row 10 times in all, then every 8th row 5 times. 37 sts.

M: 1 st at neck edge on next and every foll 10th row 3 times in all, then every 8th row 13 times. 39 sts.

L & XL: 1 st at neck edge on next and every foll 8th row 15 times in all, then every 6th row 2 times. 41 (44) sts.

Cont in patt as set until work meas 97¼ (97¼:98½:99¾:99¾) cm (38¼in) ending on WS row.

SHAPE SHOULDERS

Next row (RS): Place 11 (12:13:13:14) sts on holder, work to end in patt.
Next row: Work in patt.
Next row: Place 12 (12:13:14:15) sts on holder, work to end in patt.
Next row: Work in patt.

Next row: Work in patt, then cast off over all 35 (37:39:41:44) sts.

Work similarly for other side of neck, reversing shapings.

FINISHING

Gently block all pieces to measurements in schematic, following any care instructions on ball band.

Use a small neat backstitch on edge of work for seams. Join shoulder seams.

ARMBANDS

Measure and mark 17¾ (17¾:19:20½:20½) cm (7in) down from shoulder seam on Back and Front. Then using 3.25mm needles, with right side facing, pick up and K84 (84:90: 96:96) sts between markers. Starting on WS row, work 4cm in slip stitch rib and then cast off in rib. Repeat on other side. Join side and armband seams in one line.

NECK & HEM EDGING

Add edging around neck and hem, using crochet hook and doubled yarn. With RS facing, SS in first stitch, *miss 2 sts then DC 5 times into next stitch, miss 2 sts, SS; rep from * to end.

FLOWERS

Using photograph as a guide, attach flowers and florets randomly at the neck, waist and hem. ⊕

Tanis Gray

Mulligan Stole

Indulge yourself with this lacy scarlet stole
with a hint of retro Hollywood glamour

Tanis Gray
Mulligan Stole

SIZE

Approximately 10¼ x 60½ in (26 x 154cm)
Leaf edging approx 4¼ in (11cm) wide

YARN

This project was stitched with **Lang Yarns** Naturale, DK weight (US: sport weight) (43% baby alpaca, 23% kid mohair, 17% extrafine merino, 17% nylon); ⅞oz/25g, 104yds/95m Shade 0060 red; 4 x 25g balls

NEEDLES & ACCESSORIES

1 pair 4.5mm (UK 7/US 7) knitting needles
1 set 4.5mm (UK 7/US 7) circular needles, approx 100cm long
Stitch markers (optional)

GAUGE

12 sts and 29 rows to 10cm measured over main lace pattern using 4.5mm needles

SPECIAL ABBREVIATIONS

SSK pnso: SSK as normal, return st to left-hand needle, pass next st over, return st to right-hand needle.

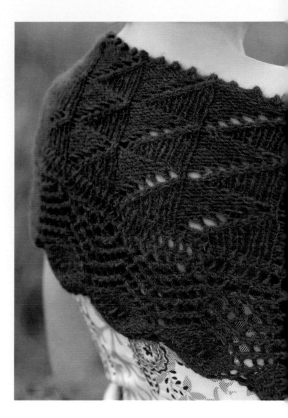

TANIS GRAY'S GORGEOUS lace stole was inspired by old Hollywood elegance and mystery. She says: "A stole draped around your neck or shoulders makes for a truly classy accessory."

A great intermediate lace project, the stole contains multiple techniques to add to your repertoire. You start by knitting an edging strip, before picking up stitches along the long edge and working the main lace pattern in the perpendicular direction.

The leaf edging changes stitch count, so keep an eye on how many stitches you have. If you're new to lace, you could use markers between each repeat of the main pattern to help you keep track.

The Lang Naturale yarn comes in a stunning selection of saturated colors, so have fun choosing your favorite!

STITCH PATTERNS

LEAF EDGING

Row 1 (RS): K2, yo, P3tog, (yo, K2tog) 5 times, yo, K1, yo, K2tog.
Row 2 (WS): P16, K2.
Row 3: K2, yo, P3tog, yo twice, SSK pnso, (yo, K2tog) 3 times, yo, K3, yo, K1. 19 sts.
Row 4: P13, (P1, K1) into double yo of previous row, P2, K2.
Row 5: K2, yo, P3tog, (yo, K2tog) 4 times, yo, K5, yo, K1. 20 sts.

Row 6: P18, K2.
Row 7: K2, yo, P3tog, yo twice, SSK pnso, (yo, K2tog) twice, yo, K7, yo, K1. 21 sts.
Row 8: P15, (P1, K1) into double yo of previous row, P2, K2.
Row 9: K2, yo, P3tog, (yo, K2tog) 3 times, yo, K9, yo, K1. 22 sts.
Row 10: P20, K2.
Row 11: K2, yo, P3tog, yo, K1, (yo, SSK) twice, yo, K4, Sl1, K2tog, psso, K4, yo, K1.
Row 12: P20, K2.
Row 13: K2, yo, P3tog, yo, (yo, SSK) 3 times, yo, K3, Sl1, K2tog, psso, K3, yo, K2tog. 21 sts.
Row 14: P15, (P1, K1) into double yo of previous row, P2, K2.
Row 15: K2, yo, P3tog, yo, K1, (yo, SSK) 3 times, yo, K2, Sl1, K2tog, psso, K2, yo, K2tog. 20 sts.
Row 16: P18, K2.
Row 17: K2, yo, P3tog, yo, (yo, SSK) 4 times, yo, K1, Sl1, K2tog, psso, K1, yo, K2tog. 19 sts.
Row 18: P13, (P1, K1) into double yo of previous row, P2, K2.
Row 19: K2, yo, P3tog, yo, K1, (yo, SSK) 4 times, yo, Sl1, K2tog, psso, yo, K2tog. 18 sts.
Row 20: P16, K2.

MAIN LACE PATTERN (MULTIPLE OF 8 STS)

Row 1 (RS): *K6, K2tog, yo; rep from * to end.

Row 2 (WS): *K1, P7; rep from * to end.
Row 3: *K5, K2tog, yo, P1; rep from * to end.
Row 4: *K2, P6; rep from * to end.
Row 5: *K4, K2tog, yo, P2; rep from * to end.
Row 6: *K3, P5; rep from * to end.
Row 7: *K3, K2tog, yo, P3; rep from * to end.
Row 8: *K4, P4; rep from * to end.
Row 9: *K2, K2tog, yo, P4; rep from * to end.
Row 10: *K5, P3; rep from * to end.
Row 11: *K1, K2tog, yo, P5; rep from * to end.
Row 12: *K6, P2; rep from * to end.
Row 13: *K2tog, yo, P6; rep from * to end.
Row 14: *K7, P1; rep from * to end.

PICOT CAST-OFF

Cast on 1 st by inserting right-hand needle between first two sts on left-hand needle. Wrap yarn around right-hand needle, pull newly made st to the front and place on left-hand needle.
Cast on 1 more st in same way.
Cast off 4 sts.
Transfer remaining st from right-hand needle to left-hand needle.

Repeat steps until all sts have been cast off.

LEAF EDGING CHART

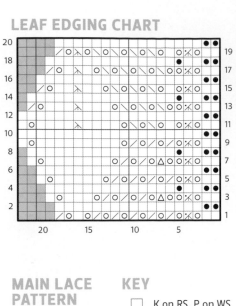

MAIN LACE PATTERN CHART

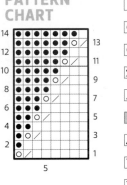

KEY

☐	K on RS, P on WS
⦿	P on RS, K on WS
O	yo
⊠	P3tog
╱	K2tog
▨	No stitch
△	SSK pnso
╲	SSK
⋌	Sl 1, K2tog, psso

STOLE

Using 4.5mm straight knitting needles, cast on 18 sts.
Purl 1 row.
Begin leaf edging, either from chart or written instructions. Work rows 1 to 20 for a total of 20 reps.
Cast off loosely knitwise.

With 4.5mm circular knitting needle, pick up 200 sts along the straight edge of the leaf edging.

Begin main lace pattern, working either from chart or written instructions, and repeating 8-stitch motif 25 times in each row.
Work rows 1–14 for a total of 3 repeats, placing st markers between repeats if needed.
Work picot cast-off to end.

Weave in all loose ends.
Block stole to measurements, following any instructions on the ball band. ✜

Melody Griffiths

Clarissa Cardigan

Extravagant frills around the body and cuffs
provide an opulent feel to this pretty cardigan

Melody Griffiths

Clarissa Cardigan

SIZE

	S	M	L	
TO FIT BUST	81-91	97-107	112-122	cm
	32-36	38-42	44-48	in
ACTUAL BUST	94½	118½	142½	cm
	37	47	56½	in
LENGTH	73	76	79	cm
	28½	30	31	in
SLEEVE SEAM	51	51	51	cm
	20	20	20	in

YARN

Maggi Knits Maggi's Linen, heavy worsted (52% cotton, 48% linen); 1¾oz/50g, 126yds/115m

PALE PINK (11)	8	11	14	x50g BALLS

NEEDLES

1 pair 5mm (UK 6/US 8) knitting needles
5mm (UK 6/US 8) circular needle, 39¼in (100cm) long
4mm (UK 8/US G) crochet hook

GAUGE

Using 5mm needles, when blocked:
9 sts of lacy diamond and faggot patt measures 2¼in (6cm)
7 sts of lacy diamond panel measures 1½in (4cm)
Edging frill measures 3½in (9cm)
Cuff frill measures 3¼in (8cm)
20 rows to 4in (10cm) over patt

SPECIAL ABBREVIATIONS

KFBF: K into front, back and front of st
PFBF: P into front, back and front of st
Chain: crochet chain (see page 11)

NOTES

To work a yo at the start of a row, simply dip the tip of the right needle under the yarn so the yarn wraps around the needle before working the first stitch on the left needle.

This yarn is made up of three strands, lightly twisted together. Take care not to miss a strand when knitting. Give the yarn an extra twist every now and then (in the right direction!) especially when casting on. Always start a new ball of yarn at the front edges – the ends will show if you start a new ball during a row.

INSPIRED BY Victorian romance, this frilled lace cardigan was designed by Melody Griffiths as a lovely garment to wear on a summer evening, to a garden party or even a wedding.

Maggi's Linen is an unusual blend of cotton and linen with three strands loosely twisted together, which really suits lacy openwork stitches.

Melody wanted to create a soft, flowing feel with the minimum of seams, so the body is worked in one piece up to the armholes. The front edges are curved slightly and the frilled edge is picked up and worked in the round, so it's flexible and there's no visible join in the pattern.

BACK AND FRONTS

Cast on 108 (144:180) sts.

SHAPE FRONT EDGES

Row 1 (RS): Yo, K8, (yo, P2tog, K7) 11 (15:19) times, KFBF. 111 (147:183) sts.
Row 2: Yo, P1, (yo, P2tog, P7) 12(16:20) times, P1, PFBF. 114 (150:186) sts.
Row 3: Yo, K2, (yo, P2tog, K3, yo, skpo,

K2) 12(16:20) times, yo, P2tog, K1, KFBF. 117 (153:189) sts.
Row 4: Yo, P4, (yo, P2tog, P7) 12(16:20) times, yo, P2tog, P2, PFBF. 120 (156:192) sts.
Row 5: Yo, K2, yo, skpo, K1, * yo, P2tog, K2, (yo, skpo) twice, K1, rep from * 11 (15:19) more times, yo, P2tog, K2, yo, skpo, KFBF. 123 (159:195) sts.
Row 6: Yo, (P7, yo, P2tog) 13 (17:21) times, P5, PFBF. 126 (162:198) sts.
Row 7: Yo, K2, (yo, skpo) 3 times, * yo, P2tog, K1, (yo, skpo) 3 times, rep from * 12 (16:20) more times, KFBF. 129 (165:201) sts.
Row 8: Yo, P10, (yo, P2tog, P7) 12 (16:20) times, yo, P2tog, P8, PFBF. 132 (168:204) sts.
Row 9: Yo, K2, * yo, P2tog, K2, (yo, skpo) twice, K1, rep from * 13 (17:21) more times, yo, P2tog, K1, KFBF. 135 (171:207) sts.
Row 10: Yo, P4, (yo, P2tog, P7) 14 (18:22) times, yo, P2tog, P2, PFBF. 138 (174:210) sts.
Row 11: Yo, K5, (yo, P2tog, K3, yo, skpo, K2) 14 (18:22) times, yo, P2tog, K4, KFBF. 141 (177:213) sts.
Row 12: Yo, (P7, yo, P2tog) 15 (19:23) times, P5, PFBF. 144 (180:216) sts.

Work lacy diamond and faggot patt straight as foll:

Row 1: (RS) K8, (yo, P2tog, K7) to last st, K1.
Row 2 and all WS rows: P8, (yo, P2tog, P7) to last st, P1.
Row 3: K4, yo, skpo, K2, (yo, P2tog, K3, yo, skpo, K2) to last st, K1.
Row 5: K3, (yo, skpo) twice, K1, * yo, P2tog, K2, (yo, skpo) twice, K1, rep from * to last st, K1.
Row 7: K2, (yo, skpo) 3 times, * yo, P2tog, K1, (yo, skpo) 3 times, rep from * to last st, K1.
Row 9: As row 5.
Row 11: As row 3.
Row 12: As row 2.
These 12 rows form lacy diamond and faggot patt.
Cont in patt for 18 more rows.

SHAPE WAIST

Row 1: Patt 28 (37:46), * skpo, K1, yo, skpo, K2tog, yo, P2tog, skpo, K1, yo, skpo, K2tog *, patt 56 (74:92), rep from * to *, patt 28 (37:46). 136 (172:208) sts.
Row 2: Patt 28 (37:46), * P5, yo, P2tog, P5 *, patt 56 (74:92), rep from * to *, patt 28 (37:46).
Row 3: Patt 28 (37:46), * K5, yo, P2tog,

Clarissa Cardigan

BLOCKING DIAGRAM

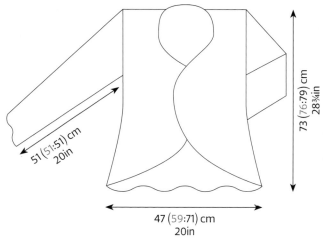

73 (76:79) cm
28¾in

51 (51:51) cm
20in

47 (59:71) cm
20in

Picking up stitches and
working in the round give a
seamless finish to the edging

K5 *, patt 56 (74:92), rep from * to *,
patt 28 (37:46).
Row 4: As row 2.
Row 5: Patt 28 (37:46), * skpo, K1,
P2tog, yo, K2tog, skpo, K1, K2tog *, patt
56 (74:92), rep from * to *, patt 28 (37:46).
128 (164:200) sts.
Row 6: Patt 28 (37:46), * P3, yo, P2tog, P3 *,
patt 56 (74:92), rep from * to *, patt
28 (37:46).
Row 7: Patt 28 (37:46), * K3, yo, P2tog,
K3 *, patt 56 (74:92), rep from * to *,
patt 28 (37:46).
Rows 8, 9 & 10: As rows 6, 7 & 6.
Row 11: Patt 28 (37:46), * (KFB) twice, K1,
yo, P2tog, (KFB) twice, K1 *, patt 56 (74:
92), rep from * to *, patt 28 (37:46).
136 (172:208) sts.
Row 12: As row 3.
Row 13: Patt 28 (37:46), * K2, yo, skpo,
K1, yo, P2tog, K2, yo, skpo, K1 *, patt
56 (74:92), rep from * to *, patt 28 (37:46).
Row 14: As row 3.
Row 15: Patt 28 (37:46), * K1, (yo, skpo)
twice, yo, P2tog, K1, (yo, skpo) twice *,
patt 56 (74:92), rep from * to *, patt
28 (37:46).
Rows 16, 17 & 18: As rows 3, 13 & 3.
Row 19: Patt 28 (37:46), * KFB, K2, KFB,
K1, yo, P2tog, KFB, K2, KFB, K1 *, patt
56 (74:92), rep from * to *, patt 28 (37:46).
144 (180:216) sts.
Cont in lacy diamond and faggot patt as
previously established, working 23 rows
straight.

SHAPE NECK AND ARMHOLES

Row 1 (RS): K1, K2tog, K5, patt to last 8 sts,
K5, skpo, K1. 142 (178:214) sts.

Row 2: Patt 1 row.
Row 3 (RS): K1, K2tog, K4, patt 20 (29:38),
* K5, cast off 6 sts, one st on right needle,
K4 *, patt 56 (74:92), rep from * to *, patt
20 (29:38), K4, skpo, K1.
This gives 31 (40:49) sts for each front and
66 (84:102) sts for the back.

LEFT FRONT

Work on first set of 31 (40:49) sts, cont
shaping neck and armhole.

Row 4 (WS): Patt 1 row.
Row 5: K1, K2tog, K2, patt 20 (29:38), K3,
skpo, K1. 29 (38:47) sts.
Row 6 and all WS rows: Working edge sts
in st st, patt as set.
Row 7: K1, K2tog, K1, patt 20 (29:38), K2,
skpo, K1. 27 (36:45) sts.
Row 9: K1, K2tog, patt 20 (29:38), K1,
skpo, K1. 25 (34:43) sts.
Row 11: K1, K2tog, K1, patt 18 (27:36),
skpo, K1. 23 (32:41) sts.
Row 13: K1, K2tog, patt 16 (25:34), K1,
skpo, K1. 21 (30:39) sts.
Row 15: K1, K2tog, K2, yo, skpo, K2, patt
9 (18:27), skpo, K1. 19 (28:37) sts.
Row 17: K1, patt 9 (18:27), K2, (yo, skpo)
twice, skpo, K1. 18 (27:36) sts.
Row 19: K1, patt 9 (18:27), K3, yo, (skpo)
twice, K1. 17 (26:35) sts.
Row 21: K1, patt 9 (18:27), K4, skpo, K1.
16 (25:34) sts.
Row 23: K1, patt 9 (18:27), K3, skpo, K1.
15 (24:33) sts.
Row 25: K1, patt 9 (18:27), K2, skpo, K1.
14 (23:32) sts.
Row 27: K1, patt 9 (18:27), K1, skpo, K1.
13 (22:31) sts.

Row 29: K1, patt 9 (18:27), skpo, K1.
12 (21:30) sts.
Cont in patt, work 15 (21:27) more rows.
Cast off.

BACK

With WS facing, rejoin yarn to center
66 (84:102) sts and cont shaping armholes.

Row 4 (WS): Patt 1 row.
Row 5: K1, K2tog, K2, patt to last 5 sts, K2,
skpo, K1. 64 (82:100) sts.
Row 6 and all WS rows: Working edge sts in
st st, patt as set.
Row 7: K1, K2tog, K1, patt to last 4 sts, K1,
skpo, K1. 62 (80:98) sts.
Row 9: K1, K2tog, patt to last 3 sts, skpo,
K1. 60 (78:96) sts. ▶

Melody Griffiths

The whole knitting
community was
saddened when in
October 2009, Melody
Griffiths passed away.
Melody learned to knit as a child, and
had a prolific design career. Working
as Assistant Knitting Editor at *Woman*
magazine, Melody went on to
commission designs for *Bella* and *Me*.
She also designed for *Woman's
Weekly*, *Simply Knitting* and of course
The Knitter. Melody had a wonderful
sense of fashion and style, as well as
an amazing understanding of hand
knitting. She is much missed.

Row 11: K1, K2tog, K1, patt to last 4 sts, K1, skpo, K1. 58 (76:94) sts.
Row 13: K1, K2tog, patt to last 3 sts, skpo, K1. 56 (74:92) sts.
Row 15: K1, K2tog, K2, yo, skpo, K2, patt to last 9 sts, K3, yo, skpo, K1, skpo, K1. 54 (72:90) sts.
Cont in patt, work 29 (35:41) more rows.
Cast off.

RIGHT FRONT

With WS facing, rejoin yarn to remaining 31 (40:49) sts and cont shaping neck and armhole.

Row 4 (WS): Patt 1 row.
Row 5: K1, K2tog, K3, patt 20 (29:38), K2, skpo, K1. 29 (38:47) sts.
Row 6 and all WS rows: Working edge sts in st st, patt as set.
Row 7: K1, K2tog, K2, patt 20 (29:38), K1, skpo, K1. 27 (36:45) sts.
Row 9: K1, K2tog, K1, patt 20 (29:38), skpo, K1. 25 (34:43) sts.
Row 11: K1, K2tog, patt 18 (27:36), K1, skpo, K1. 23 (32:41) sts.
Row 13: K1, K2tog, K1, patt 16 (25:34), skpo, K1. 21 (30:39) sts.
Row 15: K1, K2tog, patt 9 (18:27), K3, yo, (skpo, K1) twice. 19 (28:37) sts
Row 17: K1, K2tog, K1, (yo, skpo) twice, K1, patt 9 (18:27), K1. 18 (27:36) sts.
Row 19: K1, K2tog, K1, yo, skpo, K2, patt 9 (18:27), K1. 17 (26:35) sts.
Row 21: K1, K2tog, K4, patt 9 (18:27), K1. 16 (25:34) sts.
Row 23: K1, K2tog, K3, patt 9 (18:27), K1. 15 (24:33) sts.

Row 25: K1, K2tog, K2, patt 9 (18:27), K1. 14 (23:32) sts.
Row 27: K1, K2tog, K1, patt 9 (18:27), K1. 13 (22:31) sts.
Row 29: K1, K2tog, patt 9 (18:27), K1. 12 (21:30) sts.
Cont in patt, work 15 (21:27) more rows.
Cast off.

SLEEVES

Cast on 36 (45:54) sts.
Row 1 (RS): K8, (yo, P2tog, K7) to last st, K1.
This row sets patt. Cont in patt as given for back and fronts when working lacy diamond and faggot patt. Work straight, for 11 more rows.
Increase row: KFB, patt to last 2 sts, KFB, K1. 38 (47:56) sts.
Taking incs into st st, cont in patt, inc in this way at each end of 2 foll 8th rows. 42 (51:60) sts.
Taking 2 sts at each side into faggot patt, with remaining incs in st st, cont in patt, inc as before at each end of 3 foll 8th rows. 48 (57:66) sts.
Taking incs at sides into diamond lace patt, inc as before at each end of 3 foll 8th rows and on foll 4th row. 56 (65:74) sts.
Working sts at each side in st st, patt 5 rows.

SHAPE TOP

Cast off 4 sts loosely at beg of next 2 rows. 48 (57:66) sts.
Decrease row (RS): K1, K2tog, patt to last 3 sts, skpo, K1. 46 (55:64) sts.
Keeping patt correct, dec in this way at each end of next 5 RS rows. 36 (45:54) sts.
Patt 5 rows.
Next row: Cast off 3 sts, patt to last 2 sts, skpo. 32 (41:50) sts.
Next row: Cast off 3 sts, patt to last 2 sts, P2tog. 28 (37:46) sts.
Work last 2 rows again. 20 (29:38) sts.
Cast off loosely.

CUFF FRILL

With RS facing, pick up and K36 (45:54) sts from cast-on edge.
K 1 row.
Work frill as foll:
Row 1 (RS): P1, (K3, yo, P1, K3, yo, P2tog) 3(4:5) times, K3, yo, P1, K3, yo, PFB. 42 (52:62) sts.
Row 2: K1, (yo, P2tog, P3) 8 (10:12) times, K1.
Row 3: P1, (K3, yo, P2tog) 8 (10:12) times, P1.
Row 4: As row 2.
Row 5: P1, * (KFB) twice, K1, yo, P2tog, rep from * 7 (9:11) more times, P1. 58 (72:86) sts.
Row 6: K1, (yo, P2tog, P5) 8 (10:12) times, K1.
Row 7: P1, * K1, (KFB) twice, K2, yo, P2tog, rep from * 7 (9:11) more times, P1. 74 (92:110) sts.
Row 8: K1, (yo, P2tog, P7) 8 (10:12) times, K1.
Row 9: P1, * K2, (KFB) twice, K3, yo, P2tog, rep from * 7 (9:11) more times, P1. 90 (112:134) sts.
Row 10: K1, (yo, P2tog, P9) 8 (10:12) times, K1.
Row 11: P1, (K9, yo, P2tog) 8 (10:12) times, P1.
Row 12: K.
Cast-off row: Using crochet hook, cast off 2 sts, (make 3 chain, cast off 2 sts) to end.

EDGING FRILL

Matching sts, join shoulders.
Using circular needle, with RS facing and starting at faggot at center back lower edge, pick up and knit 54 (72:90) sts to front curve, 18 sts around front curve, 48 sts up right front edge, 28 (37:46) sts up right front neck, 30 sts across back neck, 28 (37:46) sts down left front neck, 48 sts down left front edge, 18 sts around front curve and 52 (70:88) sts along lower edge to start of round. 324 (378:432) sts.
Place marker for start of round.
Purl 1 round.
Round 1: (Yo, P2tog, K3, yo, P1, K3) 36 (42:48) times. 360 (420:480) sts.
Round 2: (K2tog, yo, K3) 72 (84:96) times.
Round 3: (Yo, P2tog, K3) 72 (84:96) times.
Round 4: As row 2.
Round 5: *Yo, P2tog, (KFB) twice, K1, rep from * 71 (83:95) more times. 504 (588:672) sts.
Round 6: (K2tog, yo, K5) 72 (84:96) times.
Round 7: * Yo, P2tog, K1, (KFB) twice, K2, rep from * 71 (83:95) more times. 648 (756:864) sts.
Round 8: (K2tog, yo, K7) 72 (84:96) times.
Round 9: (Yo, P2tog, K7) 72 (84:96) times.
Round 10: * K2tog, yo, K2, (KFB) twice, K3, rep from * 71 (83:95) more times. 792 (924:1056) sts.
Round 11: (Yo, P2tog, K9) 72 (84:96) times.
Round 12: (K2tog, yo, K9) 72 (84:96) times.
Rounds 13, 14 & 15: As rounds 11, 12 & 11.
P 1 round.
Cast-off row: Using crochet hook, cast off 2 sts, (make 5 chain, cast off 2 sts) to end.

FINISHING

Block according to ball band. Set in sleeves. Join sleeve seams. Darn in ends. ✪

Cozy lace

BEECHWOOD
SWEATER

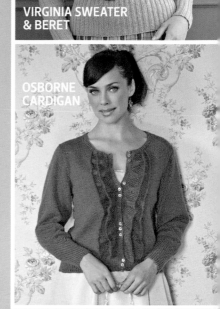

VIRGINIA SWEATER
& BERET

OSBORNE
CARDIGAN

SETTING
SUN SHAWL

CELTIC
LEAVES

Jennie Atkinson
Virginia
Sweater & Beret

Vintage-inspired sweater and matching beret
make a contemporary, feminine pairing

"THIS FLATTERING
SWEATER WAS
INSPIRED BY A
VINTAGE PATTERN"

Jennie Atkinson
Virginia Set

SIZE

		8	10	12	14	16	18	20	22	
TO FIT BUST		81	86	91	96	101	107	112	117	cm
		32	34	36	38	40	42	44	46	in
ACTUAL BUST		84	89	94	99	104	109	114	119	cm
		33	35	37	39	41	43	45	47	in
ACTUAL LENGTH		61	61	63	63	65	65	67	67	cm
		24	24	25	25	25½	25½	26½	26½	in
SLEEVE SEAM		51	51	51	51	51	51	51	51	cm
		20	20	20	20	20	20	20	20	in

YARN

This project was stitched with **Sublime**
Extra fine merino wool, 4 ply (US: fingering)
(100% extra fine merino wool); 1¾oz/50g,
191yds/175m

		8	10	12	14	16	18	20	22	
BISCUIT (06)		8	8	9	9	10	10	11	11	x50g BALLS

BERET SIZE & YARN

One size to fit average adult head.
Sublime Extra Fine Merino Wool 4 ply
Biscuit (06) 2 x 50g balls
Unfortunately, this yarn is now discontinued,
but you can easily substitute it with Sublime
Baby Cashmere Merino Silk 4 ply. We like the
pale shades of Skipper (276) and Puffin (246).

NEEDLES & ACCESSORIES

1 pair 2.75mm (UK 12/US 2) knitting needles
1 circular 2.75mm (UK 12/US 2) needle
1 pair 3.25mm (UK 10/US 3) knitting needles
1 circular 3.25mm (UK 10/US 3) needle
Set of 3.25mm (UK 10/US 3) DPNs
Belt buckle

GAUGE

28 sts by 36 rows to 4in (10cm) using 3.25mm
knitting needles over st st

THIS EXQUISITE fitted sweater is a flattering knit created by Jennie Atkinson. Jennie says: "My belted sweater design was inspired by a vintage pattern, which used a lace diamond patterning across the chest. I thought it was a beautifully simple idea and more interesting than a plain rib. I imagine it being worn with a slim, below-the-knee skirt, which conjures up images of a 1940s femme fatale, so I thought it demanded a beret!"

BACK

Using 2.75mm needles cast on 114 (122:126:134:142:146:154:162) sts.
Row 1 (RS): K2, *P2, K2; rep from * to end.
Row 2: P2, *K2, P2; rep from * to end.
Keeping rib patt correct, dec 1 st at both ends of 11th row and foll 10th row twice then every foll 8th row 3 times.
102 (110:114:122:130:134:142:150) sts.
Cont straight in rib patt for 19 rows.
Keeping patt correct, inc 1 st at both ends of next row and foll 8th row twice.
108 (116:120:128:136:140:148:156) sts.
Work 1 row ending RS facing for next row.

For sizes 12, 14 & 16 only

Work one extra row. The next row becomes your right side.

All sizes

Change to 3.25mm needles.
Next row (RS): P13 (17:19:23:27:21:25:29),
K2, *P6, K2; rep from * to last 13 (17:19:23:27:21:25:29) sts, P13 (17:19:23:27:21:25:29).
Next row: K13 (17:19:23:27:21:25:29), P2, *K6, P2; rep from * to last 13 (17:19:23:27:21:25:29) sts, K13 (17:19:23:27:21:25:29).
Cont in rib patt as set, taking all inc sts into rev st st, inc 1 st at both ends of 5th and every foll 8th row 4 (4:5:4:4:5:5:4) times.
118 (126:132:138:146:152:160:166) sts.
Work 11 (11:7:15:9:9:21:21) rows straight ending with RS facing for next row.

SHAPE ARMHOLES

Next row (RS): Cast off 6 (7:8:8:9:9:10:10) sts, patt to end.
Next row: Cast off 6 (7:8:8:9:9:10:10) sts, patt to end.
106 (112:116:122:128:134:140:146) sts.
Keeping patt correct, cast off 2 (3:3:4:4:5:5:6) sts at beg of next 2 rows.
102 (106:110:114:120:124:130:134) sts.
Dec 1 st at both ends of next 3 rows then next 2 (2:3:4:4:4:5:5) alt rows.
92 (96:98:100:106:110:114:118) sts.
Work one row straight, ending with RS facing for next row.

DIAMOND PATTERN

Row 1 (RS): P4 (6:7:8:11:5:7:9), *K2tog, yo, SSK, P4; rep from * to last 0 (2:3:4:7:1:3:5) sts, P0 (2:3:4:7:1:3:5).
Row 2: K4 (6:7:8:11:5:7:9), *P1, KFB, P1, K4: rep from * to last 0 (2:3:4:7:1:3:5) sts, K0 (2:3:4:7:1:3:5).
Row 3: P3 (5:6:7:10:4:6:8), *K2tog, yo, K2, yo, SSK, P2; rep from * to last 1
(3:4:5:8:2:4:6) sts, P1 (3:4:5:8:2:4:6).
Row 4: K3 (5:6:7:10:4:6:8), *P6, K2; rep from * to last 1 (3:4:5:8:2:4:6) sts, K1 (3:4:5:8:2:4:6).
Row 5: P2 (4:5:6:9:3:5:7), *(K2tog, yo) twice, SSK, yo, SSK; rep from * to last 2 (4:5:6:9:3:5:7) sts, P2 (4:5:6:9:3:5:7).
Row 6: K2 (4:5:6:9:3:5:7), *P3, KFB, P3; rep from * to last 2 (4:5:6:9:3:5:7) sts, K2 (4:5:6:9:3:5:7).
Row 7: P2 (4:5:6:9:3:5:7), *(yo, SSK) twice, K2tog, yo, K2tog; rep from * to last 2 (4:5:6:9:3:5:7) sts, yo, P2 (4:5:6:9:3:5:7).
Row 8: K2 (4:5:6:9:3:5:7), K1 tbl, P6, *KFB, P6; rep from * to last 3 (5:6:7:10:4:6:8) sts, K1 tbl, K2 (4:5:6:9:3:5:7).
Row 9: P3 (5:6:7:10:4:6:8), *yo, Sl 1, K2tog, psso, yo, K3tog, yo, P2; rep from * to last 1 (3:4:5:8:2:4:6) sts, P1 (3:4:5:8:2:4:6).
Row 10: K3 (5:6:7:10:4:6:8), *K1 tbl, P1, KFB, P1, K1 tbl, K2; rep from * to last 1 (3:4:5:8:2:4:6) sts, K1 (3:4:5:8:2:4:6) sts.
Row 11: P4 (6:7:8:11:5:7:9), *yo, SSK, K2tog, yo, P4; rep from * to last 0 (2:3:4:7:1:3:5) sts, P0 (2:3:4:7:1:3:5).
Row 12: K4 (6:7:8:11:5:7:9), *K1 tbl, P2, K1 tbl, K4; rep from * to last 0 (2:3:4:7:1:3:5) sts, K0 (2:3:4:7:1:3:5).
Row 13: P5 (7:8:9:12:6:8:10), K2, *P6, K2; rep from * to last 5 (7:8:9:12:6:8:10) sts, P5 (7:8:9:12:6:8:10).
Row 14: K5 (7:8:9:12:6:8:10), P2, *K6, P2; rep from * to last 5 (7:8:9:12:6:8:10), P5 (7:8:9:12:6:8:10).
***Rep last 2 rows 23 (23:24:23:25:25:25:25) more times.

BLOCKING DIAGRAM

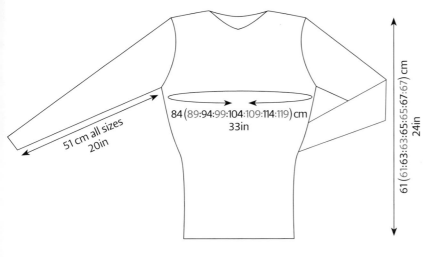

51 cm all sizes
20in

84 (89:94:99:104:109:114:119) cm
33in

61 (61:63:63:65:65:67:67) cm
24in

SHOULDERS AND BACK NECK

Next row (RS): Patt 31 (33:34:35:36:38:40: 42) sts. Turn. (Slip rem sts to stitch holder.)
Next row: Work 2tog, patt to end.
Next row: Cast off 10 (10:11:11:11:12:13:13) sts.
Next row: Work 2tog, patt to end.
Next row: Cast off 9 (10:10:11:11:12:12:13) sts.
Next row: Work 2tog, patt to end.
Next row: Cast off rem 9 (10:10:10:11:11: 12:13) sts.
With RS facing return to sts on holder. Keep center 30 (30:30:30:34:34:34:34) sts on holder and rejoin yarn to rem 31 (33:34:35:36:38:40:42) sts and complete to match first side, reversing shapings.

FRONT

Work as given for Back to ***
Rep last 2 rows 7 (7:7:7:5:5:5:5) more times ending with RS facing for next row.

SHAPE NECK

Next row (RS): Patt 45 (47:48:49:52:54:56: 58) sts. Turn. (Slip rem sts on to a holder.)
Next row: Patt to end.
Keeping patt correct, dec 1 st at neck edge of next and every foll alt row until you have 29 (31:32:33:34:36:38:40) sts.
Work one row straight.
Next row (RS): Cast off 10 (10:11:11:11:12: 13:13) sts, patt to end.
Next row: Work 2tog, patt to end.
Next row: Cast off 9 (10:10:11:11:12:12:13) sts, patt to end.

Next row: Patt 9 (10:10:10:11:11:12:13) sts.
Next row: Cast off rem 9 (10:10:10:11:11: 12:13) sts.
With RS facing return to rem sts on holder, leave next (center) 2 sts on holder, rejoin yarn to rem 45 (47:48:49:52:54:56:58) sts. Work to match first side of neck, reversing shapings.

SLEEVES

Using 2.75mm needles cast on 50 (50:54:54:58:58:62:62) sts.
Row 1 (RS): K2, *P2, K2; rep from * to end.
Row 2: P2, *K2, P2; rep from * to end.
Keeping rib patt correct, inc 1 st at both ends of 11th row and every foll 10th row until 60 (60:64:64:68:68:72:72) sts.
Change to 3.25mm needles.
Row 1 (RS): P5 (5:7:7:9:9:11:11), K2, *P6, K2; rep from * to last 5 (5:7:7:9:9:11:11) sts, P5 (5:7:7:9:9:11:11).
Row 2: K5 (5:7:7:9:9:11:11), P2, *K6, P2: rep from * to last 5 (5:7:7:9:9:11:11) sts, K5 (5:7:7:9:9:11:11).
Cont in rib patt as set, working all inc sts in rev st st, inc 1 st at both ends of 3rd row and every foll 8th row to 82 (82:86:86:90:90: 94:94) sts, then every foll 4th row to 108 (108:112:112:116:116:120:120) sts.
Cont until sleeve meas 20in (51cm) ending with RS facing for next row.

SLEEVEHEAD

Next row (RS): Cast off 6 (7:8:8:9:9:10:10) sts, patt to end.
Next row: Cast off 6 (7:8:8:9:9:10:10) sts,

patt to end.
Cast off 2 (3:3:4:4:5:5:6) sts at beg next 2 rows. 92 (88:90:88:90:88:90:88) sts.

Size 8 only
Dec 1 st at both ends of next row and foll 2 alt rows. 86 sts.
Work 1 row.

Sizes 10–22 only
Dec 1 st at both ends of next row and foll 4th row. – (84:86:84:86:84:86:84) sts.
Work 3 rows straight.

All sizes
Cont in Diamond Pattern while shaping sleevehead thus:
Row 1: P2tog, P15 (14:15:14:15:14:15:14), *K2tog, yo, SSK, P4; rep from * to last 13 (12:13:12:13:12:13:12) sts, P11 (10:11:10: 11:10:11:10), P2tog.
77 (75:77:75:77:75:77:75) sts.
Row 2: K16 (15:16:15:16:15:16:15), *P1, KFB, P1, K4; rep from * to last 12 (11:12:11:12:11: 12:11) sts, K12 (11:12:11:12:11:12:11).
84 (82:84:82:84:82:84:82) sts.
Row 3: P15 (14:15:14:15:14:15:14), *K2tog, yo, K2, yo, SSK, P2; rep from * to last 13 (12:13:12:13:12:13:12) sts, P13 (12:13:12:13:12:13:12).
Row 4: K15 (14:15:14:15:14:15:14), *P6, K2; rep from * to last 13 (12:13:12:13:12:13:12) sts, P13 (12:13:12:13:12:13:12).
Row 5: P2tog, P12 (11:12:11:12:11:12:11) *(K2tog, yo) twice, SSK, yo, SSK; rep from * to last 14 (13:14:13:14:13:14:13) sts, P12 ▶

(11:12:11:12:11:12:11), P2tog.
75 (73:75:73:75:73:75:73) sts.
Row 6: K13 (12:13:12:13:12:13:12), *P3, KFB, P3; rep from * to last 13 (12:13:12:13:12:13: 12) sts, K13 (12:13:12:13:12:13:12). 82 (80:82:80:82:80:82:80) sts.
Row 7: P13 (12:13:12:13:12:13:12), *(yo, SSK) twice, K2tog, yo, K2tog; rep from * to last 13 (12:13:12:13:12:13:12) sts, yo, P13 (12:13:12:13:12:13:12). 76 (74:76:74:76:74:76:74) sts.
Row 8: K13 (12:13:12:13:12:13:12), K1 tbl, P6, * KFB, P6; rep from * to last 14 (13:14:13:14: 13:14:13) sts, K1 tbl, K13 (12:13:12:13:12: 13:12). 82 (80:82:80:82:80:82:80) sts.
Row 9: P2tog, P12 (11:12:11:12:11:12:11), *yo, Sl 1, K2tog, psso, yo, K3tog, yo, P2; rep from * to last 12 (11:12:11:12:11:12:11) sts, P10 (9:10:9:10:9:10:9), P2tog. 73 (71:73:71:73:71:73:71) sts.
Row 10: K13 (12:13:12:13:12:13:12), *K1 tbl, P1, KFB, P1, K1 tbl, K2; rep from * to last 11 (10:11:10:11:10:11:10), K11 (10:11:10:11: 10:11:10). 80 (78:80:78:80:78:80:78) sts.
Row 11: P14 (13:14:13:14:13:14:13), *yo, SSK, K2tog, yo, P4; rep from * to last 10 (9:10:9:10:9:10:9) sts, P10 (9:10:9:10:9:10:9).
Row 12: K14 (13:14:13:14:13:14:13), *K1 tbl, P2, K1 tbl, K4; rep from * to last 10 (9:10:9:10:9:10:9) sts, K10 (9:10:9:10:9:10:9).
Row 13: P2tog, P13 (12:13:12:13:12:13:12), K2, *P6, K2; rep from * to last 15 (14:15:14: 15:14:15:14) sts, P13 (12:13:12:13:12:13:12), P2tog. 78 (76:78:76:78:76:78:76) sts.
Row 14: K14 (13:14:13:14:13:14:13), P2, *K6, P2; rep from * to last 14 (13:14:13:14:13:14: 13) sts, K14 (13:14:13:14:13:14:13).
Keeping rib as set by last 2 rows, dec 1 st at each end of next and 4 (6:11:10:14:13: 14:13) foll alt rows, then dec 1 st at each end of every row 10 (7:3:3:0:0:0:0) times. 48 sts.
Next row: Cast off 4 sts at beg next 2 rows.
Next row: Cast off 8 sts at beg next 2 rows.
Next row: Cast off rem 24 sts.

NECK TRIM

Join shoulder seams.
With RS of work facing, using 3.25mm circular needle, starting at left shoulder seam, pick up and K36 (36:40:40:44:44: 48:48) sts down left front neck, K2tog at center front from holder, pick up and K36 (36:40:40:44:44:48:48) sts up right front neck, 4 sts from right back neck, patt across 30 (30:30:30:34:34:34:34) sts from back neck st holder, and 4 sts from left back neck. 111 (111:119:119:131:131:139:139) sts. Work in the round as foll:
Rnd 1: P2, (K2, P2) 8 (8:9:9:10:10:11:11) times, K2tog tbl, K center st, K2tog, *P2,

K2; rep from * to end.
Rnd 2: Rib to within 2 sts of center st, K2tog tbl, K center st, K2tog, rib to end.
Rep last round 2 more times.
Using 5mm needle cast off in rib.

BELT

Using 2.75mm needles cast on 15 sts. Work in K1, P1, rib until belt measures desired length. Dec at both ends on every row until 3 sts rem, K3tog and pull yarn through st.

FINISHING

Sew side seams, sew sleeve seams, sew sleeves into garment. Make i-cord belt loops in side seams.

Jennie Atkinson
Virginia Beret

Using 2.75mm circular needle cast on 146 sts. Taking care not to twist sts, join to work in the round. Mark beg of round.
Rnd 1: K2, *P2, K2; rep from * to end.
Rep last round 7 more times.
Next rnd: Rib 10 sts, M1,* rib 6, M1; rep from * to last 10 sts, rib to end. 168 sts.

Change to 3.25mm circular needle.
Rnd 1: *P2, K2, P2; rep from * to end.
Rep this round 4 times more.
Rnd 6: *P1, inc in next st purlwise, K2, P2; rep from * to end. 196 sts.
Rnd 7: *P3, K2, P2; rep from * to end.
Rep last round 3 times more.
Rnd 11: *P3, K2, P1, inc in next st purl wise; rep from * to end. 224 sts.
Rnd 12: *P3, K2, P3; rep from * to end.
Rnd 13: (Diamond pattern) *P2, K2tog, yo, SSK, P2; rep from * to end. 196 sts.

Rnd 14: *P2, K1, KFB, K1, P2; rep from * to end. 224 sts.
Rnd 15: *P1, K2tog, yo, K2, yo, SSK, P1; rep from * to end.
Rnd 16: *P1, K6, P1; rep from * to end.
Rnd 17: *(K2tog, yo) twice, SSK, yo, SSK; rep from * to end. 196 sts.
Rnd 18: *K3, KFB, K3; rep from * to end.
Rnd 19: *(yo, SSK) twice, K2tog, yo, K2tog; rep from * to end. 196 sts.
Rnd 20: *KFB, K6; rep from * to end. 224 sts.
Rnd 21: Remove marker, Sl 1, replace marker, *P1, yo, Sl 1, K2tog, psso, yo, K3tog, yo, P1; rep from * to end. 196 sts. Continue with new position for start of round marker.
Rnd 22: *P2, K1, KFB, K1, P2; rep from * to end. 224 sts.
Rnd 23: *P2, yo, SSK, K2tog, yo, P2; rep from * to end.
Rnd 24: *P3, K2, P3; rep from * to end.
Rep last round 4 times more.
Rnd 29: *P3, Sl 1, K1, psso, P3; rep from * to end. 196 sts.
Rnd 30: *P3, K1, P3; rep from * to end.
Rep this last round 7 times more.
Rnd 38: P3, K1, *P2tog, P2, P2tog, K1, P6, K1; rep from * to last 10 sts, P2tog, P2, P2tog, K1, P3. 168 sts.
Rnd 39: P3, K1, *P4, K1, P6, K1; rep from * to last 8 sts, P4, K1, P3.
Rep last round 7 times more.
Rnd 47: P3, K1, *(P2tog) twice, K1, P6, K1; rep from * to last 8 sts, (P2tog) twice, K1, P3. 140 sts.
Rnd 48: P3, K1, *P2, K1, P6, K1; rep from * to last 6 sts, P2, K1, P3.
Rep last round 5 times more.
Rnd 54: P3, K1, *P2tog, K1, P6, K1; rep from * to last 6 sts, P2tog, K1, P3. 126 sts.
Rnd 55: P3, K1, *P1, K1, P6, K1; rep from * to last 5 sts, P1, K1, P3.
Rep last round 5 times more.
Rnd 61: P3, *Sl 1, K2tog, psso, P6; rep from * to last 6 sts, Sl 1, K2tog, psso, P3. 98 sts.
Rnd 62: P3, *K1, P6; rep from * to last 4 sts, K1, P3.
Rep last round once more.
Rnd 64: *P1, P2tog, K1, P2tog, P1; rep from * to end. 70 sts.
Rnd 65: *P2, K1, P2; rep from * to end.
Rnd 66: *P2tog, K1, P2tog; rep from * to end. 42 sts.
Rnd 67: *P1, K1, P1; rep from * to end.
Rnd 68: P1, *K1, P2tog; rep from * to end, using first st to make last P2tog. 28 sts.
Rnd 69: *P2tog; rep from * to end. 14 sts.
Break yarn and thread through rem sts, pull tight and fasten off securely. ✪

Marie Wallin

Osborne Cardigan

This beautiful cardigan with a softly-rounded
neck has delicate lace ruffles to add detail

SIZE

SIZE	8	10	12	14	16	18	20	22	
TO FIT BUST	81	86	91	97	102	107	112	117	cm
	32	34	36	38	40	42	44	46	in
ACTUAL BUST	88	92	96	100	105	110	115	120	cm
	34½	36	38	39½	41½	43½	45½	47	in
ACTUAL LENGTH	55	56	56	57	58	59	60	60	cm
	21½	22	22	22½	23	23	23½	23½	in
SLEEVE SEAM	45	45	45	45	45	45	45	45	cm
	17½	17½	17½	17½	17½	17½	17½	17½	in

YARN

This project was stitched with the following yarns.
Rowan Pure Wool 4 Ply, (US: fingering) (100% superwash wool); 1¾oz/50g, 175yds/160m

A RASPBERRY (428)	8	8	9	9	10	10	11	11	x50g BALLS

Rowan Kidsilk Haze, lace weight (70% super kid mohair, 30% silk); ⅞oz/25g, 230yds/210m

B BLUSHES (583)	1	1	1	1	1	1	1	1	x25g BALLS

NEEDLES

1 pair 2.75mm (UK 12/US 2) knitting needles
1 pair 3.25mm (UK 10/US 3) knitting needles

ACCESSORIES

12 x 11mm buttons

GAUGE

28 sts and 36 rows to 10cm over stockinette stitch using 3.25mm needles and yarn A

Marie Wallin
Osborne Cardigan

MARIE WALLIN has combined two different yarns for the body of this cardigan with ruffle lace trim. The cardigan itself is a classic shape, featuring deep rib cuffs and buttons clustered in groups of three to offer a different look. But it is the stunning double-layer ruffle down the front edges that really enhances this design.

Marie says: "The idea behind the Osborne cardigan has come from the classic and vintage styles of the 1920s and 1930s country set. This slightly eccentric trend with a contemporary edge was also the main inspiration behind the 'Heritage' story in *Rowan Magazine 46*."

She also explains: "The design is knitted in Rowan Pure Wool 4ply yarn to give a vintage feel, which is then complemented and brought up to date with the addition of the pretty lace frill edging in Rowan Kidsilk Haze."

BACK

Using 2.75mm needles and yarn A cast on 123 (129:135:141:147:155:161:169) sts.
Row 1 (RS): K1, *P1, K1, rep from * to end.
Row 2: P1, *K1, P1, rep from * to end.
These 2 rows form rib.
Work in rib for a further 23 rows, ending with WS facing for next row.
Change to 3.25mm needles.

Beg with a P row, work in st st as folls:
Cont straight until back meas 34cm, ending with RS facing for next row.

SHAPE ARMHOLES

Cast off 5 (5:6:6:8:8:9:9) sts at beg of next 2 rows.
113 (119:123:129:131:139:143:151) sts.
Dec 1 st at each end of next 5 (5:5:5: 4:5:5:6) rows and 4 (5:5:6:6:7:7:8) foll alt rows.
95 (99:103:107:111:115:119:123) sts.
Cont straight until armhole meas 20 (20½:21:21½:23:24:25:25) cm (8in) ending with RS facing for next row.

SHAPE BACK NECK AND SHOULDERS

Next row (RS): Work 29 (30:31:32:33: 34:35:36) sts and turn, leaving rem sts on a holder.
Work each side of neck separately.
Cast off 3 sts at beg of next and foll alt row, AT SAME TIME cast off 8 (8:8:9:9: 9:10:10) sts at beg of 2nd and foll alt row. 7 (8:9:8:9:10:9:10) sts.
Work 1 row.
Cast off rem 7 (8:9:8:9:10:9:10) sts.

With RS facing, rejoin yarn to rem sts, cast off center 37 (39:41:43:45:47:49:51) sts K to end.
29 (30:31:32:33:34:35:36) sts.
Complete to match first side, reversing shapings.

LEFT FRONT

Using 2.75mm needles and yarn A cast on 58 (62:64:68:70:74:78:82) sts.
Row 1 (RS): *K1, P1, rep from * to end.
Row 2: *K1, P1, rep from * to end.
These 2 rows form rib.
Work in rib for a further 23 rows, ending with WS facing for next row.
Change to 3.25mm needles.
Beg with a P row, work in st st as folls:
Cont straight until Front matches Back to beg of armhole shaping, ending with RS facing for next row.

SHAPE ARMHOLE

Cast off 5 (5:6:6:8:8:9:9) sts at beg of next row.
53 (57:58:62:62:66:69:73) sts.
Work 1 row.
Dec 1 st at armhole edge of foll 5 (5:5:5:4:5:5:6) rows and 4 (5:5:6:6:7:7:8) foll alt rows.
44 (47:48:51:52:54:57:59) sts.
Cont straight until Front meas 41cm from cast-on edge, ending with WS facing for next row.

SHAPE FRONT NECK

Cast off 10 sts at beg of next row.
34 (37:38:41:42:44:47:49) sts.
Work 1 row.
Dec 1 st at neck edge of next 4 (5:5:7:7:7:11:13) rows, then on 7 (8:8:8:9:7:6) foll alt rows.

BLOCKING DIAGRAM

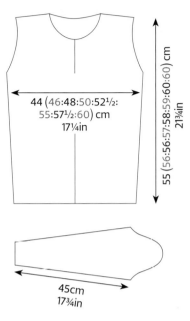

44 (46:48:50:52½:
55:57½:60) cm
17¼in

55 (56:56:57:58:59:60:60) cm
21¾in

45cm
17¾in

23 (24:25:26:27:28:29:30) sts.
Work straight until armhole matches
Back to beg of shoulder shaping, ending
with RS facing for next row.

SHAPE SHOULDER
Cast off 8 (8:8:9:9:9:10:10) at beg of next
and foll alt row.
7 (8:9:8:9:10:9:10) sts. Work 1 row.
Cast off rem 7 (8:9:8:9:10:9:10) sts.

RIGHT FRONT
Using 2.75mm needles and yarn A cast
on 58 (62:64:68:70:74:78:82) sts.
Row 1 (RS): *P1, K1, rep from * to end.
Row 2: *P1, K1, rep from * to end.
These 2 rows form rib.
Work in rib for a further 23 rows,
ending with WS facing for next row.
Change to 3.25mm needles.
Work to match Left Front reversing
shapings.

SLEEVES
Using 2.75mm needles and yarn A
cast on 57 (57:59:59:61:61:63:63) sts.
Work in rib as given for Back for
26 rows, ending with RS facing for
next row.
Cont in rib, inc 1 st at each end of next
and 8 foll 4th rows.
75 (75:77:77:79:79:81:81) sts.
Work 3 rows in rib.
Inc 1 st at beg of next row.

76 (76:78:78:80:80:82:82) sts.
Work 1 row in rib, ending with RS
facing for next row.
Change to 3.25mm needles.
Beg with a K row, work in st st, shaping
sides as folls:

Sizes 12–22 only
Inc 1 st at each end of 3rd and
– (–:3:3:12:12:22:22) foll 4th rows.
– (–:86:86:106:106:128:128) sts.
Work three rows.

Sizes 8–18 only
Inc 1 st at each end of 3rd and 14
(14:12:12:6:6:–:–) foll 6th rows.
106 (106:112:112:120:120:–:–) sts.

All sizes
Cont straight until sleeve meas
approx 45cm, ending with RS facing
for next row.

SHAPE TOP
Cast off 5 (5:6:6:8:8:9:9) sts at beg of
next 2 rows.
96 (96:100:100:104:104:110:110) sts.
Dec 1 st at each end of next and foll 6
rows, then on 13 (13:15:15:17:17:20:20)
foll alt rows, then on foll 3 rows, ending
with RS facing for next row. 50 sts.
Cast off 8 sts at beg of next 4 rows.
18 sts.
Work 1 row with RS facing for next row.
Cast off rem 18 sts.

FINISHING
Press carefully following instructions
on ball band.
Sew shoulder seams.

NECKBAND
With RS facing, using 2.75mm needles
and yarn A, beg and ending at front
opening edges, pick up and knit 43
(46:46:48:48:50:51:52) sts up right side
of neck, 57 (59:61:63:65:67:69:71) sts
from back, then 43 (46:46:48:48:50:
51:52) sts down left side.
143 (151:153:159:161:167:171:175) sts.
Row 1 (WS): P1 *K1, P1, rep from * to end.
Row 2 (RS): K1 *P1, K1, rep from * to end.
These 2 rows form rib.
Work in rib for a further 3 rows ending
with RS facing for next row.
Cast off in rib.

BUTTON BAND
With RS facing, using 2.75mm needles

and yarn A, pick up and knit 165 sts
evenly down left front opening edge,
from cast-off edge of neckband to
cast-on edge.
Work in rib as given for neckband for
5 rows ending with RS facing for
next row.
Cast off in rib.

BUTTONHOLE BAND
With RS facing, using 2.75mm needles
and yarn A, pick up and knit 165 sts
evenly up right front opening edge,
from cast-on edge to cast-off edge
of neckband.
Work in rib as given for neckband for
2 rows ending with WS facing for
next row.
Row 3 (WS): *Rib 1, cast off 3 sts, rib 4 sts,
cast off 3 sts, rib 4 sts, cast off 3, rib 31; * rep
from * to * twice more, cast off 3 sts, rib 4
sts, cast off 3 sts, rib 4 sts, cast off 3, rib 1.
Row 4 (RS): Rib to end, casting on 3 sts
over those cast off on previous row.
Work in rib for a further row.
Cast off in rib.

FRONT LACE EDGING (make 4 alike)
Using 2.75mm needles and yarn B, cast
on 104 sts.
Row 1 and every alt row (WS): K2, P to last
2 sts, K2.
Row 2 (RS): *K7, yo, Sl1, K1, psso, yo, K4;
rep from * to end. 112 sts.
Row 4: *K6, (yo, Sl1, K1, psso) twice, yo,
K4; rep from * to end. 120 sts.
Row 6: *K5, (yo, Sl1, K1, psso) 3 times, yo,
K4; rep from * to end. 128 sts.
Row 8: *K4, (yo, Sl1, K1, psso) 4 times, yo,
K4; rep from * to end. 136 sts.
Row 10: *K3, (yo, Sl1, K1, psso) 5 times, yo,
K4; rep from * to end. 144 sts.
Row 12: *K4, (yo, Sl1, K1, psso) 5 times,
K2tog, K2; rep from * to end. 136 sts.
Row 14: *K5, (yo, Sl1, K1, psso) 4 times,
K2tog, K2; rep from * to end. 128 sts.
Row 16: *K6, (yo, Sl1, K1, psso) 3 times,
K2tog, K2; rep from * to end. 120 sts.
Row 18: *K7, (yo, Sl1, K1, psso) twice,
K2tog, K2; rep from * to end. 112 sts.
Row 20: *K8, yo, Sl1, K1, psso, K2tog, K2;
rep from * to end. 104 sts.
Cast off.

Set in sleeves using the set-in method.
Attach front lace edging ¾in (2cm) in
from front opening edges and at
opening edges before button bands. Do
not attach to ribbing. ⊕

Anniken Allis

Setting Sun Shawl

This exquisite feather-light lace shawl
adds a touch of glamour and warmth
to an elegant outfit

Anniken Allis

Setting Sun Shawl

SIZE

Diameter: 160cm (63in)

YARN

This project was stitched with **Malabrigo** Lace, lace weight (100% baby merino); 1¾oz/50g, 470yds/430m Bergamota (94) 5 x 50g skeins

NEEDLES & ACCESSORIES

1 set 3.25mm (UK 10/US 3) double-pointed needles (DPNs)
2 sets 3.25mm (UK 10/US 3) circular needles, 23½in (60cm) & 39¼in (100cm) long
8 stitch markers

GAUGE

2 pattern repeats of chart A to measure 3½in (9cm) wide and 4¾in (12cm) long after blocking, using 3.25mm needles

PATTERN NOTES

This circular shawl is divided into 8 triangular sections. We recommend placing a stitch marker between each section.
The shawl is worked from the center outwards with edging knitted on at the end. Start with double-pointed needles and change to circular needles once you have too many stitches for the DPNs. Change to longer circular needles as needed.
Any circular cast-on method can be used. Anniken used the Turkish cast-on, which creates a closed center.

CHART NOTES

All charts except for the edging chart show only patterned rounds. Even-numbered rounds are knitted throughout.

CREATED IN a fiery hand-dyed crimson color, we're positive that this vibrant sunset shawl will dispel the gloom from the dreariest of days.

The sheer size of the shawl makes it something of a commitment, but because it's knitted from the center outwards, it will grow really quickly at first. The super-soft 100% baby merino wool from Malabrigo is a joy to work with, making this an ideal project for working on, cozied up by the fire.

TURKISH CAST-ON

The following instructions explain how to cast on four stitches using the Turkish method. (This creates a closed center for this circular shawl, which is worked from the center outwards.)
Hold two DPNs horizontally and parallel to each other in your left hand. Make a slip knot and place on the bottom needle. Wrap the yarn under needle, up back of needle and round and down in front of the needles. Repeat once more. There are now 2 loops on needles. Knit through the loops on the top needle. Turn, do not knit the slip knot (just slip it off the needle) and knit through the loops of the second needle.

SHAWL

Using 3.25mm DPNs, cast on 4 sts using Turkish cast-on. Divide your sts onto four DPNs (one st on each needle).
Round 1: *K1, yo; rep from *to end of round. 8 sts.
Round 2: K8.

Each of these 8 sts will now form the point of each of the 8 sections of the shawl.

Round 1: Reading all rows of chart from right to left, work row 1 from Set-up chart, repeating the row 8 times in each round, one repeat in each of the 8 sections.
Round 2: Knit.
Continue to work from Set-up chart, until all 47 rows of chart are complete, knitting all even numbered rounds (which are not shown on chart). 200 sts.
Round 48: Knit.

Now work all 24 rows of chart A 3 times (even-numbered rows are not shown on chart, but are knitted as before).
After each repeat of the 24 rows, the marked part of the chart will need to be repeated an extra time in each section. 488 sts (61 sts in each of the 8 sections).

Now work all 46 rows of chart B once (knitting even-numbered rows). 672 sts (84 sts in each of the 8 sections).

The knitted-on edging is worked back and forth

BLOCKING DIAGRAM

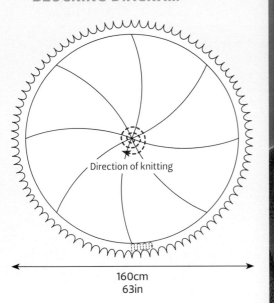

Direction of knitting

160cm
63in

Now work all 71 rows of chart C once, repeating marked part of chart twice in each section, and working each row of chart 8 times (once in each section). 960 sts (120 sts in each section). Leave sts on needle.

EDGING

Using 3.25mm needles, cast on 8 sts using any provisional cast-on method.

With RS of shawl facing, work row 1 of the Edging chart, knitting the last st of edging and one st from shawl together.

Continue working around the shawl, knitting the last edging stitch together with a shawl stitch at the end of each RS row of edging.

Once all 96 repeats of edging pattern have been worked, undo provisional cast-on and place cast-on sts on a double-pointed needle.
Graft the two ends of the edging together using Kitchener stitch.

FINISHING

Weave in all loose ends, but don't trim them. Soak shawl in lukewarm water until thoroughly wet. Carefully squeeze out excess water with a big towel.

Prepare a large space and stretch shawl to size and pin in place. Each point of the edging needs to be pinned out. Leave shawl to dry and unpin when completely dry. Trim loose ends neatly. ⊕　▶

The eight lace panels of the shawl radiate out from the center

In detail
Knitted-on edgings

It is common to see lace shawls finished with a knitted-on edging rather than casting off stitches. This is beneficial because a strip of knitting has more stretch than a cast-off edge, so the lace can be blocked more fully.

The edging is knitted back and forth perpendicular to the body of the shawl, and at the end of each RS row, the final edging stitch is knitted together with a stitch from the body of the shawl. This means that a stitch of the body is effectively cast off each time this happens. As the edging is also joined to the shawl as you knit, no seaming is required, making it a flawless finish.

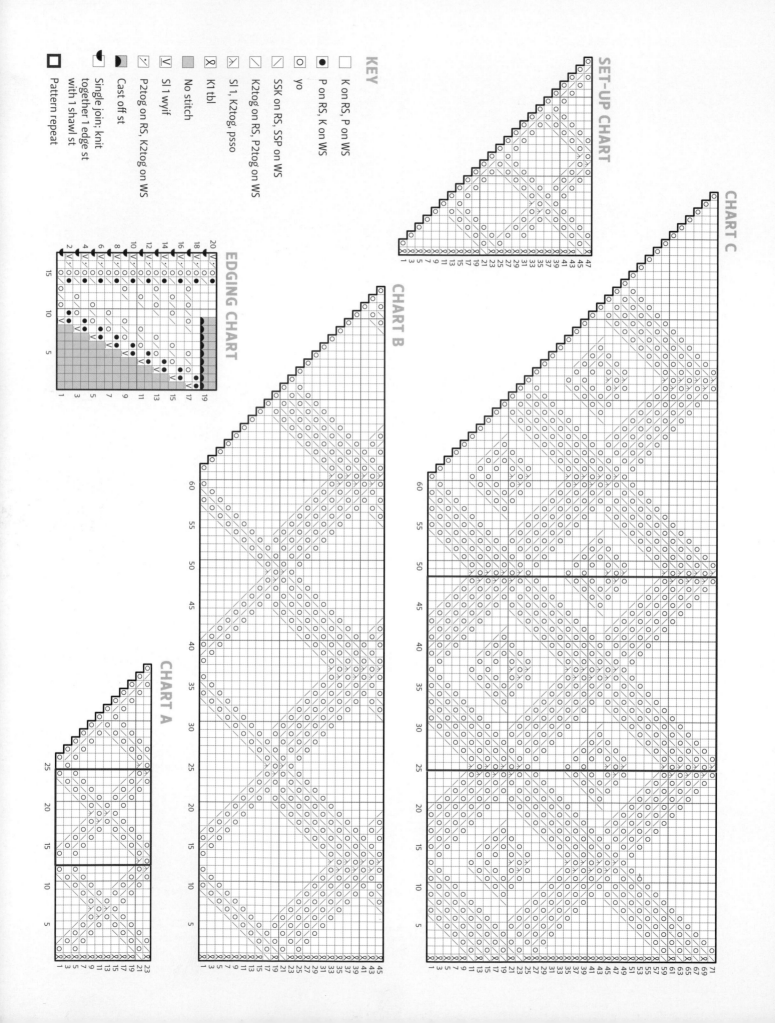

KEY

- ☐ K on RS, P on WS
- ● P on RS, K on WS
- ○ yo
- ╱ SSK on RS, SSP on WS
- ╲ K2tog on RS, P2tog on WS
- ⋏ Sl1, K2tog, psso
- ⋉ K1 tbl
- ▨ No stitch
- Ⅴ Sl 1 wyif
- ▨ Cast off st
- ☑ P2tog on RS, K2tog on WS
- ◗ Single join; knit together 1 edge st with 1 shawl st
- ☐ Pattern repeat

SET-UP CHART

CHART C

CHART B

EDGING CHART

CHART A

Sarah Hatton

Beechwood Sweater

Pretty crewneck sweater is an interesting knit
with its sideways panels of delicate leaves

SIZE

	8	10	12	14	16	18	20	22	
TO FIT BUST	81	86	91	96	101	107	112	117	cm
	32	34	36	38	40	42	44	46	in
ACTUAL BUST	90	94	98	104	110	116	122	128	cm
	35	37	39	41	43	46	48	50	in
ACTUAL LENGTH	51	51	51	54	54	56	56	58	cm
	20	20	20	21½	21½	22	22	23	in
SLEEVE SEAM	45	45	46	46	47	47	47	47	cm
	17½	17½	18	18	18½	18½	18½	18½	in

YARN

This project was stitched with **Regia** Silk, 4ply weight (US: fingering) (55% wool, 25% polyamide, 20% silk); 1¾oz/50g, 219yds/200m

ARKTIKBLAU (00055)	6	6	7	7	8	8	9	9	x50g BALLS

Unfortunately, the Arktikblau color is now discontinued, but there are plenty of other colors available and we like Blue Grey (00052).

NEEDLES

1 pair 2.75mm (UK 12/US 2) needles
1 pair 3.25mm (UK 10/US 3) needles

GAUGE

28 sts and 36 rows to 4in (10cm) measured over st st using 3.25mm needles. Leaf panel meas 4¾in (12cm) wide, and each repeat meas 2¼in (7cm) from leaf tip to leaf tip.

Sarah Hatton
Beechwood Sweater

THIS BEAUTIFUL design by Sarah Hatton takes a classic women's garment and gives it an interesting twist by inserting a panel of sideways-running leaves across the upper chest.

Two separate leaf panels are knitted, one for the front and one for the back. The rest of each piece is then picked up and knitted from the row-end edges of the panel. This is shown in both charted and written forms, so this pattern gives you a chance to practice with charts if you don't normally use them.

Regia Silk is used for a lustrous, super-soft effect. The yarn contains 25% polyamide so it's a hard-wearing blend, and is also machine washable.

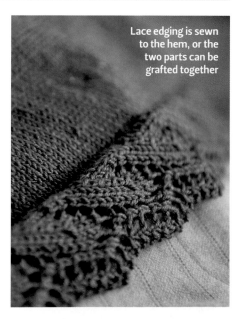

Lace edging is sewn to the hem, or the two parts can be grafted together

CABLE LEAF PANEL (Make 2)

This panel is also shown in the chart. Using 3.25mm needles, cast on 38 sts.
Row 1 (WS): (K1, P2) 3 times, K2, P5, K4, P3, K6, (P2, K1) 3 times.
Row 2: P1, T2R, P1, K2tog, yfrn, P1, T2R, P4, P2tog, KFB, K2, P4, K2, yfwd, K1, yfwd, K2, P2, T2R, P1, K2tog, yfrn, P1, T2R, P1.
Row 3: (K1, P2) 3 times, K2, P7, K4, P2, K1, P1, K5, (P2, K1) 3 times.
Row 4: P1, T2R, P1, yfwd, skpo, P1, T2R, P3, P2tog, K1, PFB, K2, P4, K3, yfwd, K1, yfwd, K3, P2, T2R, P1, yfwd, skpo, P1, T2R, P1.
Row 5: (K1, P2) 3 times, K2, P9, K4, P2, K2, P1, K4, (P2, K1) 3 times.
Row 6: P1, T2R, P1, K2tog, yfrn, P1, T2R, P2, P2tog, K1, PFB, P1, K2, P4, skpo, K5, K2tog, P2, T2R, P1, K2tog, yfrn, P1, T2R, P1.
Row 7: (K1, P2) 3 times, K2, P7, K4, P2, K3, P1, K3, (P2, K1) 3 times.
Row 8: P1, T2R, P1, yfwd, skpo, P1, T2R, P1, P2tog, K1, PFB, P2, K2, P4, skpo, K3, K2tog, P2, T2R, P1, yfwd, skpo, P1, T2R, P1.
Row 9: (K1, P2) 3 times, K2, P5, K4, P2, K4, P1, K2, (P2, K1) 3 times.
Row 10: P1, T2R, P1, K2tog, yfrn, P1, T2R, P2, yfwd, K1, yfwd, P4, K2, P4, skpo, K1, K2tog, P2, T2R, P1, K2tog, yfrn, P1, T2R, P1.
Row 11: (K1, P2) 3 times, K2, P3, K4, P2, K4, P3, K2, (P2, K1) 3 times.
Row 12: P1, T2R, P1, yfwd, skpo, P1, T2R, P2, (K1, yfwd) twice, K1, P4, K1, M1, K1, P2tog, P2, Sl 2 sts knitwise together, K1, p2sso, P2, T2R, P1, yfwd, skpo, P1, T2R, P1.
Row 13: (K1, P2) 3 times, K6, P3, K4, P5, K2, (P2, K1) 3 times.
Row 14: P1, T2R, P1, K2tog, yfrn, P1, T2R,

P2, K2, yfwd, K1, yfwd, K2, P4, K1, KFB, K1, P2tog, P4, T2R, P1, K2tog, yfwd, P1, T2R, P1.
Row 15: (K1, P2) 3 times, K5, P1, K1, P2, K4, P7, K2, (P2, K1) 3 times.
Row 16: P1, T2R, P1, yfwd, skpo, P1, T2R, P2, K3, yfwd, K1, yfwd, K3, P4, K2, PFB, K1, P2tog, P3, T2R, P1, yfwd, skpo, P1, T2R, P1.
Row 17: (K1, P2) 3 times, K4, P1, K2, P2, K4, P9, K2, (P2, K1) 3 times.
Row 18: P1, T2R, P1, K2tog, yfrn, P1, T2R, P2, skpo, K5, K2tog, P4, K2, P1, PFB, K1, P2tog, P2, T2R, P1, K2tog, yfrn, P1, T2R, P2.
Row 19: (K1, P2) 3 times, K3, P1, K3, P2, K4, P7, K2, (P2, K1) 3 times.
Row 20: P1, T2R, P1, yfwd, skpo, P1, T2R, P2, skpo, K3, K2tog, P4, K2, P2, PFB, K1, P2tog, P1, T2R, P1, yfwd, skpo, P1, T2R, P1.
Row 21: (K1, P2) 3 times, K2, P1, K4, P2, K4, P5, K2, (P2, K1) 3 times.
Row 22: P1, T2R, P1, K2tog, yfrn, P1, T2R, P2, skpo, K1, K2tog, P4, K2, P4, yfwd, K1, yfwd, P2, T2R, P1, K2tog, yfwd, P1, T2R, P1.
Row 23: (K1, P2) 3 times, K2, P3, K4, P2, K4, P3, K2, (P2, K1) 3 times.
Row 24: P1, T2R, P1, yfwd, skpo, P1, T2R, P2, Sl 2 sts knitwise together, K1, p2sso, P2, P2tog, K1, M1, K1, P4, (K1, yfwd) twice, K1, P2, T2R, P1, yfwd, skpo, P1, T2R, P1.
These 24 rows set patt. Cont in patt until work meas 39 (41:43:46:49:52:55:58)cm (15½in), ending with RS facing for next row. Cast off.

UPPER BACK PANEL

Using 2.75mm needles pick up and knit 110 (116:122:130:138:146:156:164) sts evenly along right edge of first cable leaf panel.

SPECIAL ABBREVIATIONS

T2R: Work into front of second st but do not take off needle, knit into front of the first st and slip both sts off needle together.

p2sso: Pass 2 slipped stitches over.

yfrn: Yarn forward and round: bring the yarn forward and all the way around the needle until it is forward again.

CABLE LEAF CHART

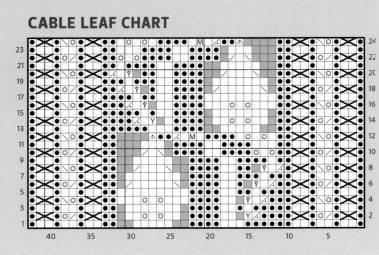

KEY

☐	K on RS, P on WS
●	P on RS, K on WS
⊙	yo
▨	no stitch (ignore these squares and move straight to next instruction)
⟍	Sl 1, K1, psso
⟋	K2tog
Y	KFB
M	Make one
⟋	P2tog
Ẏ	PFB
⋀	Sl 2 sts knitwise together, K1, p2sso
⧓	T2R

BLOCKING DIAGRAM

45 (47:49:52:55:58:61:64) cm
17¾in

45 (45:46:46:47:47:47:47) cm
17¾in

51 (51:51:54:54:56:56:58) cm
20in

Cuffs are finished with a row of eyelets

Change to 3.25mm needles, beg with a P row and working in st st throughout work 13 (13:15:15:17:17:19:19) rows, ending with RS facing for next row.

SHAPE BACK NECK AND SHOULDER

Next row (RS): Cast off 9 (10:11:12:13: 14:16:17) sts, knit until there are 24 (26:28:31:32:35:38:41) sts on needle, turn and leave rem sts on a holder. Cont on these 24 (26:28:31:32:35:38:41) sts only.

Next row: Cast off 3 sts, purl to end.

Next row: Cast off 9 (10:11:12:13:14:16:17) sts, knit to end.

Next row: Cast off 3 sts, purl to end.
Cast off rem 9 (10:11:13:13:15:16:18) sts. With RS facing, rejoin yarn to rem sts, cast off center 44 (44:44:44:48:48:48: 48) sts, knit to end.
Complete to match first side of neck, reversing all shaping.

LOWER BACK PANEL

Using 2.75mm needles pick up and knit

110 (116:122:130:138:146:156:164) sts evenly along left side of first cable leaf panel.

Change to 3.25mm needles, beg with a P row and working in st st throughout cont as foll:
Work 1 row.

Next row: K2, M1, knit to last 2 sts, M1, K2. This row sets armhole increases.
Inc 1 st as set at each end of 3 foll alt rows and on 4 foll rows.
126 (132:138:146:154:162:172:180) sts.
Cont without shaping until work meas 34 (34:34:34:36:36:36:36) cm from start of shoulder shaping, ending with RS facing for next row.

Next row: K2, skpo, knit to last 4 sts, K2tog, K2.
This row sets waist decrease.
Dec 1 st as set at each end of 2 foll 8th rows.
120 (126:132:140:148:156:166:174) sts.
Work 11 rows without shaping.

Next row: K2, M1, knit to last 2 sts, M1, K2. This row sets waist increase.

Inc 1 st as set at each end of 2 foll 6th rows.
126 (132:138:146:154:162:172:180) sts.
Cont straight until work meas 51 (51:51:54: 54:56:56:58) cm from shoulder, ending with RS facing for next row.
Cast off.

UPPER FRONT PANEL

Using 2.75mm needles pick up and knit 110 (116:122:130:138:146:156:164) sts evenly along right edge of second cable leaf panel.

Change to 3.25mm needles, beg with a P row and working in st st throughout cont as foll:

SHAPE FRONT NECK

Next row: K35 (38:41:45:49:53:58:62) sts, turn and leave rem sts on a holder.
Work each side of neck separately.
Dec 1 st at neck edge of next 6 (6:6:6:8:8:8:8) rows, then on 2 foll alt rows.
27 (30:33:37:39:43:48:52) sts.
Work 1 (1:3:3:5:5:7:7) rows without shaping, ending with RS facing for next row. ▶

In detail
Chart or written?

Most knitters have a preference for either charted or written instructions. There are benefits to working from a chart, though. The chart should represent how the pattern will look when finished, so you can see that the areas of reverse stockinette stitch are shown as dark dots on the chart. The eyelet holes are also easy to spot on the chart, because they are shown as circles. If you regularly compare your work to the chart, you can easily spot and correct mistakes.

Check the progress of your lace pattern against the chart

SHAPE SHOULDERS

Cast off 9 (10:11:12:13:14:16:17) sts at beg of next and foll alt row.
Work 1 row.
Cast off rem 9 (10:11:13:13:15:16:18) sts.
Leave center 40 sts on a holder, rejoin yarn to rem sts and knit to end.
Complete to match first side of neck, reversing all shapings.

LOWER FRONT PANEL

Work as given for lower back panel.

SLEEVES (Make 2)

Using 2.75mm needles cast on 61 (61:67:67:67:67:73:73) sts.
Row 1 (RS): P2, K3, *P3, K3; rep from * to last 2 sts, P2.
Row 2: K2, *P3, K3; rep from * to last 5 sts, P3, K2.
These 2 rows set rib.
Work 14 rows more in rib.
Next row: P2, K2tog, yfwd, K1, *P3, K2tog, yfwd, K1; rep from * to last 2 sts, P2.
Next row: As row 2, dec – (–:2:2:–:–:2:2) sts evenly across row.
61 (61:65:65:67:67:71:71) sts.

Change to 3.25mm needles, beg with a K row and working in st st throughout, inc 1 st at each end of 5th and 2 (2:5:5:11:11:17:17) foll 8th (6th:6th:6th:6th:6th:6th:6th) rows then on every foll 10th (8th:8th:8th:8th:8th:8th:8th) row to 89 (95:101:101:107:107:113:117) sts.
Cont without shaping until sleeve meas 45 (45:46:46:47:47:46:46) cm ending with RS facing for next row.
Next row: K2, skpo, knit to last 4 sts, K2tog, K2.
Next row: P2, P2tog, purl to last 4 sts, P2tog tbl, P2.
These 2 rows set decreases.

Dec 1 st at each end of next 3 rows, then on 3 foll alt rows.
73 (79:85:85:91:91:97:101) sts.
Work 1 row, ending with RS facing for next row.
Cast off.

FINISHING

Join right shoulder seam.

NECKBAND

With RS facing, using 2.75mm needles, pick up and knit 11 (11:14:14:15:15:18:18) sts evenly down left side of neck, 40 sts from holder at front neck, 12 (12:15:15:16:16:19:19) sts up right side of neck, 7 sts down side of back neck, 44 (44:44:44:48:48:48:48) sts from back neck and 7 sts up side of back neck. 121 (121:127:127:133:133:139:139) sts.
Next row (WS): K2, *P3, K3; rep from * to last 5 sts, P3, K2.
Next row: P2, K2tog, yfwd, K1, *P3, K2tog, yfwd, K1; rep from * to last 2 sts, P2.
Next row: K2, *P3, K3; rep from * to last 5 sts, P3, K2.
Next row: P2, K3, *P3, K3; rep from * to last 2 sts, P2.
Last 2 rows set rib.
Work 9 rows more in rib.
Cast off in rib.
Join left shoulder and neckband seam.
Join side seams.

HEM EDGING

Using 3.25mm needles cast on 13 sts.
Row 1 and every foll alt row (WS): K2, P to last 2 sts, K2.
Row 2: Sl 1, K3, yfwd, K5, yfwd, K2tog, yfwd, K2. 15 sts.
Row 4: Sl 1, K4, Sl 1, K2tog, psso, K2, (yfwd, K2tog) twice, K1. 13 sts.
Row 6: Sl 1, K3, skpo, K2, (yfwd, K2tog) twice, K1. 12 sts.
Row 8: Sl 1, K2, skpo, K2, (yfwd, K2tog) twice, K1. 11 sts.
Row 10: Sl 1, K1, skpo, K2, (yfwd, K2tog) twice, K1. 10 sts.
Row 12: K1, skpo, K2, yfwd, K1, yfwd, K2tog, yfwd, K2. 11 sts.
Row 14: Sl 1, (K3, yfwd) twice, K2tog, yfwd, K2. 13 sts.
These 14 rows set pattern.

Cont in patt until border fits around hem edge, ending with row 14 and RS facing for next row.

Cast off, sewing in position at same time. Alternatively, you may wish to cast on using a contrast yarn and once you have worked to length, graft the ends together.

Join sleeve seams and sew in position. Pin out and cover with damp cloths and leave until dry. ⊕

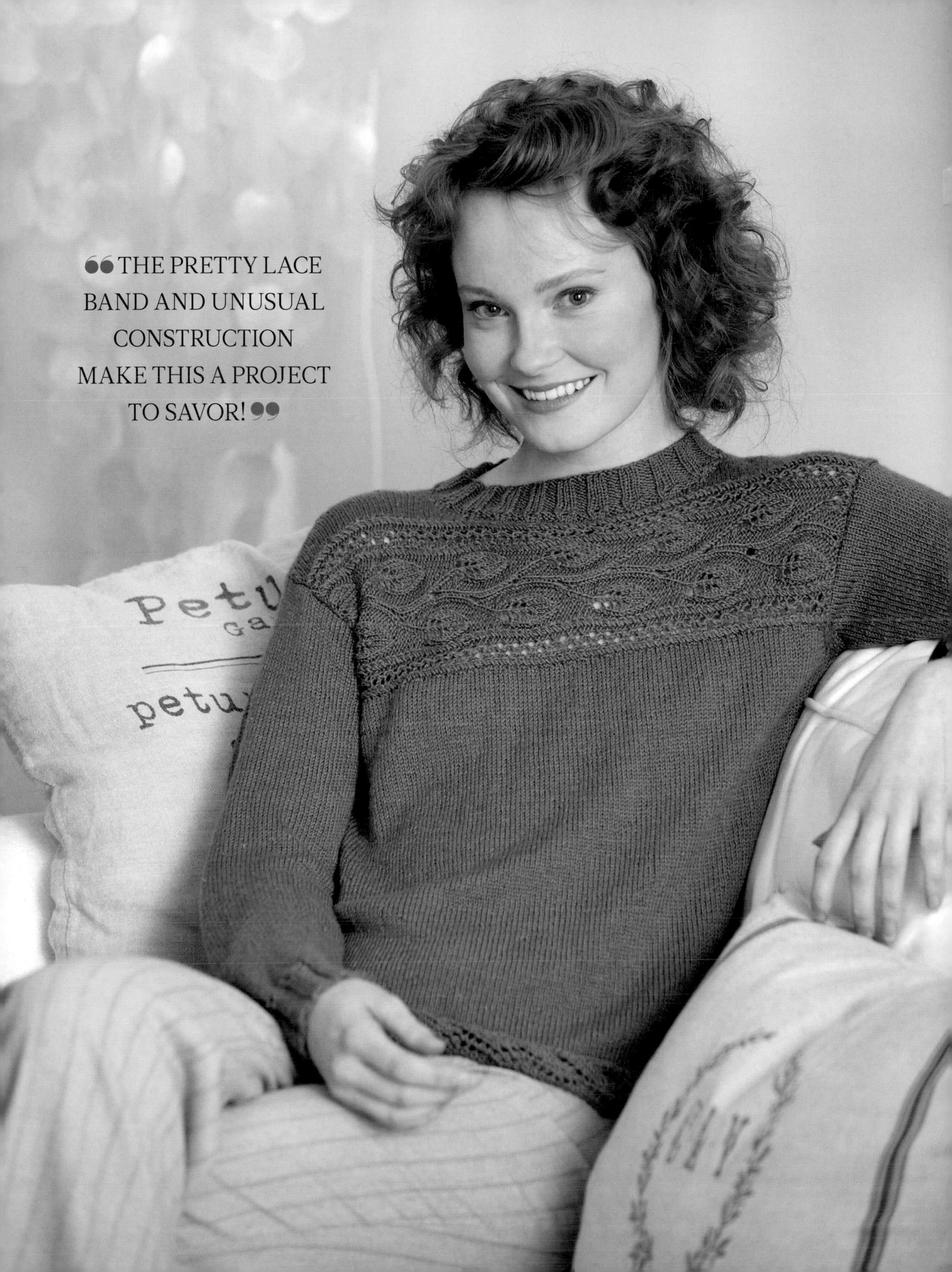

❝THE PRETTY LACE BAND AND UNUSUAL CONSTRUCTION MAKE THIS A PROJECT TO SAVOR!❞

Judy Furlong

Celtic Leaves

Elegant draping and pleats top off this
rectangular shawl, which incorporates lace
patterning and cablework

Judy Furlong
Celtic Leaves

SIZE
Width: 25½in (65cm)
Length (adjustable): 65in (165cm)
If a longer shawl is preferred, more yarn will be required. One ball of yarn (40g) is sufficient for 7–7¾in (18–20cm) of main section of shawl.

YARN
This project was stitched with **Zealana** Kiwi 2ply lace weight (40% fine NZ merino, 30% organic cotton, 30% possum); 1½oz/40g, 218yds/199m
Papura (06) 8 x 40g balls

NEEDLES & ACCESSORIES
1 pair 3.25mm (UK 10/ US 3) knitting needles (a circular needle may be preferred for the box pleat sections due to the large number of sts)
2 cable or double-pointed needles
6 stitch markers

GAUGE
27 sts and 30 rows to 4in (10cm) using 3.25mm needles over lace pattern, after dressing

SPECIAL ABBREVIATIONS
C7B: Cable 7 back: slip the next 4 sts onto a cable needle, hold at back of work, K3 from LH needle, slip the purl st on the cable needle onto the LH needle and purl this st, K3 from the cable needle.
C7F: Cable 7 forward: slip the next 4 sts onto a cable needle, hold at front of work, K3 from LH needle, slip the purl st on the cable needle onto the LH needle and purl this st, K3 from the cable needle.
yb: Take yarn to back under RH needle (no inc).
yrn: Yarn round needle; take yarn over the top and back under the right needle (1 inc).
yfwd: Yarn forward over needle (1 inc).

WITH STUNNING DEFINITION to the stitch patterns, this shawl will not only make for an interesting knit, but a fabulous accessory for your wardrobe or home. Judy Furlong is the designer of this piece and she explains: "This shawl is straightforward to knit and combines some classic stitch patterns especially chosen to complement each other."

The shawl is simplified by the fact that the center and inner panel stitch pattern repeats are 20 rows, the borders are 10 rows, and the lattice is the same on every row. Judy adds: "So it will be quick to pick up the pattern repeats."

She also says: "Special techniques include grafting and the Channel Island cast on, which is not essential but does add an interesting detail."

STITCH PATTERNS
CHANNEL ISLAND CAST ON
Tie a slip knot in one end of a doubled length of yarn (allowing approximately 0.5cm of doubled yarn per stitch), and slip it onto a RH needle.
* Hold the double yarn in the palm of the Left Hand, bring it out between the first finger and thumb and wind it right round the thumb counter-clockwise.
Bring the single thickness yarn (attached to ball) under and over the RH needle and knit a st where the doubled yarn crosses itself on the thumb.

Carefully pull up the doubled yarn to form a little knot. This produces two sts (3 sts now on the RH needle including the original slip knot).

Repeat from *, casting on two sts at a time, until the required number of sts are on the RH needle.

BOX PLEATS
1st half of pleat: Slip first 10 sts onto cable needle. Slip next 10 sts (5 purl sts, followed by 5 knit sts) onto second cable needle. Hold both these needles at the back of work. Fold the fabric so that the second cable needle is lying behind and alongside the LH needle and the first cable needle is lying alongside the second (three needles lying side by side). K3tog by inserting tip of RH needle into the first st of the LH needle, the first cable needle, then second cable needle, knit all 3 sts together. Repeat 9 more times.

2nd half of pleat: Slip first 10 sts onto cable needle and keep at front of work. Slip next 10 sts (5 knit sts, followed by 5 purl sts) onto second cable needle. Fold the fabric so that the first cable needle is at front of work, the second is sandwiched between the first cable needle and the LH needle which is at back of work. K3tog by inserting tip of RH needle into the first st of the first cable needle, the second cable then the LH needle, knit all 3 sts together. Repeat 9 more times.

RIGHT BORDER
Note: As the st counts in this panel change, it is easiest to check at end of 10th row.

Row 1: K3, yfwd, K1 tbl, K2tog, P1, skpo, K1 tbl, yfwd, K2, bring yarn to front, yrn, P2tog, yrn, P2tog, K1.
Row 2: K3, bring yarn to front, yrn, P2tog, yrn, P2tog, P3, K1, P3, K3.
Rows 3 & 4: Rep last 2 rows once more.
Row 5: K4, yfwd, K2tog, P1, skpo, yfwd, K1 tbl, yfwd, K2, bring yarn to front, yrn, P2tog, yrn, P2tog, K1. 18 sts.
Row 6: K3, bring yarn to front, yrn, P2tog, yrn, P2tog , P4, K1, P2, K4.
Row 7: K5, yfwd, K3tog, yfwd, K1 tbl, K1, K1 tbl, yfwd, K2, bring yarn to front, yrn, P2tog, yrn, P2tog, K1. 19 sts.
Row 8: K3, bring yarn to front, yrn, P2tog, yrn, P2tog, P7, K5.
Row 9: Cast off 4 sts, K2 (3 sts on RH needle), yfwd, K1 tbl, K3, K1 tbl, yfwd, K2, bring yarn to front, yrn, P2tog, yrn, P2tog, K1. 17 sts.
Row 10: K3, bring yarn to front, yrn, P2tog, yrn, P2tog, P7, K3.

INNER PANEL (left and right the same)
Row 1: K1, *yfwd, K2, skpo, P7, K2tog, K2, yfwd, K1; rep from *.
Row 2: P5, K7, P9, K7, P5.
Row 3: K2, yfwd, K2, skpo, P5, K2tog, K2, yfwd, K2tog, yfwd, K1, yfwd, K2, skpo, P5, K2tog, K2, yfwd, K2.

Channel Island cast-on gives a decorative effect to the edge of the box pleats

Row 4: P6, K5, P11, K5, P6.
Row 5: *K2tog, yfwd, K1, yfwd, K2, skpo, P3, K2tog, K2, yfwd, K2tog, yfwd; rep from * to last st, K1.
Row 6: P7, K3, P13, K3, P7.
Row 7: K1, K2tog, yfwd, K1, yfwd, K2, skpo, P1, K2tog, K2, yfwd, (K2tog, yfwd) 3 times, K1, yfwd, K2, skpo, P1, K2tog, K2, yfwd, K2tog, yfwd, K2.
Row 8: P8, K1, P15, K1, P8.
Row 9: P5, C7B, P9, C7B, P5.
Row 10: K5, P3, K1, P3, K9, P3, K1, P3, K5.
Row 11: P4, K2tog, K2, yfwd, K1, yfwd, K2, skpo, P7, K2tog, K2, yfwd, K1, yfwd, K2, skpo, P4.
Row 12: K4, P9, K7, P9, K4.
Row 13: P3, K2tog, K2, yfwd, K2tog, yfwd, K1, yfwd, K2, skpo, P5, K2tog, K2, yfwd, K2tog, yfwd, K1, yfwd, K2, skpo, P3.
Row 14: K3, P11, K5, P11, K3.
Row 15: P2, K2tog, K2, yfwd, (K2tog, yfwd) twice, K1, yfwd, K2, skpo, P3, K2tog, K2, yfwd, (K2tog, yfwd) twice, K1, yfwd, K2, skpo, P2.
Row 16: K2, P13, K3, P13, K2.
Row 17: P1, *K2tog, K2, yfwd, (K2tog, yfwd) 3 times, K1, yfwd, K2, skpo, P1; rep from * to marker.
Row 18: K1, *P15, K1; rep from * to marker.
Row 19: P1, K3, P9, C7F, P9, K3, P1.
Row 20: K1, P3, K9, P3, K1, P3, K9, P3, K1.

LATTICE (8 sts)
Every row: K3, bring yarn to front, yrn, P2tog, yrn, P2tog, K1.

CENTER PANEL
Row 1: K1, *yfwd, skpo, P7, K2tog, yfwd, K1; rep from* to marker.
Row 2: P3, K7, *P5, K7; rep from *to last 3 sts before marker, P3.
Row 3: K1, *yfwd, K1, skpo, P5, K2tog, K1, yfwd, K1; rep from * to marker.
Row 4: P4, K5, *P7, K5; rep from * to last 4 sts before marker, P4.
Row 5: K1, *yfwd, K2, skpo, P3, K2tog, K2, yfwd, K1; rep from * to marker.
Row 6: P5, K3, *P9, K3; rep from * to last 5 sts before marker, P5.
Row 7: K1, *yfwd, K3, skpo, P1, K2tog, K3, yfwd, K1; rep from * to marker.
Row 8: P6, K1, *P11, K1; rep from * to last 6 sts before marker, P6.
Row 9: K1, *yfwd, K4, Sl1, K2tog, psso, K4, yfwd, K1; rep from * to marker.
Row 10: Purl.
Row 11: P4, K2tog, yfwd, K1, yfwd, skpo, *P7, K2tog, yfwd, K1, yfwd, skpo; rep from * to last 4 sts before marker, P4.
Row 12: K4, P5, *K7, P5; rep from * to last 4 sts before marker, K4.
Row 13: P3, K2tog, K1, (yfwd, K1) twice, skpo, *P5, K2tog, K1, (yfwd, K1) twice, skpo; rep from * to last 3 sts before marker, P3.
Row 14: K3, P7, *K5, P7; rep from * to last 3 sts before marker, K3.
Row 15: P2, K2tog, K2, yfwd, K1, yfwd, K2, skpo, *P3, K2tog, K2, yfwd, K1, yfwd, K2, skpo; rep from * to last 2 sts before marker, P2.
Row 16: K2, P9, *K3, P9; rep from * to last 2 sts before marker, K2.

Row 17: P1, *K2tog, K3, yfwd, K1, yfwd, K3, skpo, P1; rep from * to marker.
Row 18: K1, *P11, K1; rep from * to marker.
Row 19: K2tog, K4, yfwd, K1, yfwd, K4, *Sl1, K2tog, psso, K4, yfwd, K1, yfwd, K4; rep from * to last 2 sts before marker, skpo.
Row 20: Purl.

LEFT BORDER
Note: As the st counts in this panel change, it is easiest to check at end of 10th row.

Row 1: K3, bring yarn to front, yrn, P2tog, yrn, P2tog, yo, K1 tbl, K2tog, P1, skpo, K1 tbl, yfwd, K3.
Row 2: K3, P3, K1, P3, K2, bring yarn to front, yrn, P2tog, yrn, P2tog, K1.
Rows 3 & 4: Rep last 2 rows once more.
Row 5: K3, bring yarn to front, yrn, P2tog, yrn, P2tog, yo, K1 tbl, yfwd, K2tog, P1, skpo, yfwd, K4. 18 sts.
Row 6: K4, P2, K1, P4, K2, bring yarn to front, yrn, P2tog, yrn, P2tog, K1.
Row 7: K3, bring yarn to front, yrn, P2tog, yrn, P2tog, yo, K1 tbl, K1, K1 tbl, yfwd, Sl1, K2tog, psso, yfwd, K5. 19 sts.
Row 8: K5, P7, K2, bring yarn to front, yrn, P2tog, yrn, P2tog, K1.
Row 9: K3, bring yarn to front, yrn, P2tog, yrn, P2tog, yo, K1 tbl, K3, K1 tbl, yfwd, K7. 21 sts.
Row 10: Cast off 4 sts, K2 (3 sts on RH needle), P7, K2, bring yarn to front, yrn, P2tog, yrn, P2tog, K1. 17 sts.

▶

CENTER PANEL CHART

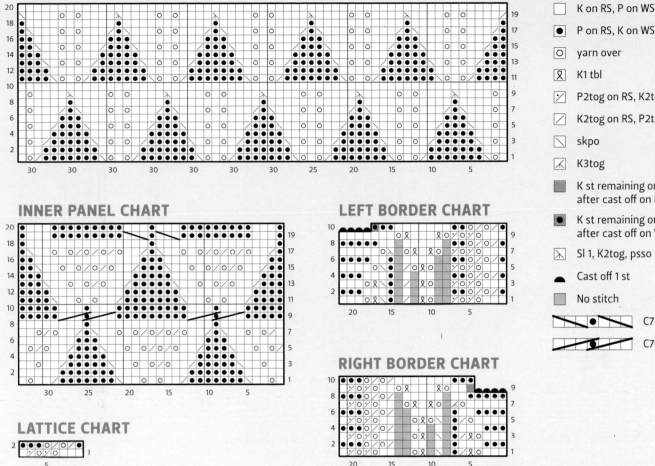

INNER PANEL CHART

LEFT BORDER CHART

RIGHT BORDER CHART

LATTICE CHART

KEY

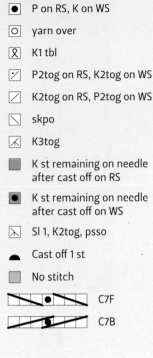

☐	K on RS, P on WS
●	P on RS, K on WS
○	yarn over
	K1 tbl
	P2tog on RS, K2tog on WS
	K2tog on RS, P2tog on WS
	skpo
	K3tog
■	K st remaining on needle after cast off on RS
	K st remaining on needle after cast off on WS
	Sl 1, K2tog, psso
	Cast off 1 st
	No stitch
	C7F
	C7B

SHAWL

FIRST BOX-PLEATED BORDER

Cast on 547 sts, using Channel Island method (allowing approximately 275cm of doubled yarn).

Row 1: Knit.
Row 2: K1, P2tog tbl, yo, K270, K2tog, knit to last 3 sts, bring yarn to front, yrn, P2tog, K1. 546 sts.
Row 3: K3, P15, K30, *P30, K30, repeat from * to last 18 sts, P15, K3.
Row 4: K1, P2tog tbl, yo, K15, P30, *K30, P30, repeat from * to last 18 sts, K15, bring yarn to front, yrn, P2tog, K1.

Repeat the last 2 rows 9 more times (22 rows from cast-on edge).

MAKING BOX PLEATS

Row 23: K3, make 9 box pleats, K3. 186 sts.
Row 24: K1, P2tog tbl, yo, K17, (K2tog, K16) 8 times, K2tog, K17, bring yarn to front, yrn, P2tog, K1. 177 sts.
Row 25: Knit.

Row 26: K1, P2tog tbl, yo, K14, pm, K33, pm, K8, pm, K61, pm, K8, pm, K33, pm, K14, bring yarn to front, yrn, P2tog, K1.

MAIN SECTION

Placing panels:
Row 1: Work Row 1 of all panels as follows: Right Edge Border (17 sts), slm, Inner Panel (33 sts), slm, Lattice (8 sts), slm, Center Panel (61 sts), slm, Lattice (8 sts), slm, Inner Panel (33 sts), slm, Left Edge Border (17 sts).

Continue as established, repeating the panels until 438 rows (21 repeats and 18 rows of Center and Inner panels, 43 repeats and 8 rows of Right and Left Edge borders) have been worked.

Row 439: Work Right Edge Border Row 9, slm, P1, K12, C7F, K12, P1, slm, work Lattice, slm, Center Panel Row 19, slm, Lattice, slm, P1, K12, C7F, K12, P1, slm, work Left Edge Border Row 9.
Row 440: Cast off 4 sts, P2tog tbl, yo, Knit

to last 3 sts removing markers, bring yarn to front, yrn, P2tog, K1. 177 sts.

Break off yarn and leave these sts on a spare needle ready to graft to Second Box-Pleated Border.

SECOND BOX-PLEATED BORDER

Work as for First Box-Pleated Border until Row 24 has been completed. Break off yarn leaving sufficient to graft to Main Section.

FINISHING

Graft Second Box-Pleated Border to Main Section, using Kitchener stitch.
Darn in loose ends.

DRESSING

Soak for a few minutes in lukewarm water or wash according to manufacturer's instructions. Gently roll in a clean towel to remove excess water. Spread out according to measurements and allow to dry. ⊕

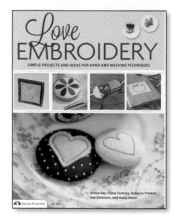
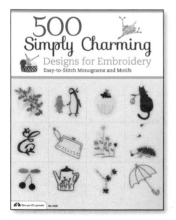

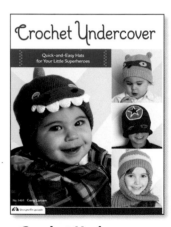

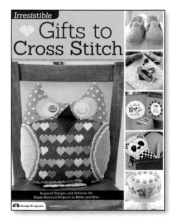